Good News
for
Alienated Catholics

with reflection questions
for teachers and preachers

Fr. Henry Fehren

Resource Publications, Inc.
San Jose, California

Editorial director: Kenneth Guentert
Managing editor: Elizabeth J. Asborno

Reprint Department
Resource Publications, Inc.
160 E. Virginia Street #290
San Jose, CA 95112-5876

Library of Congress Cataloging in Publication Data
Fehren, Henry.
    Good news for alienated Catholics : with reflection
questions for teachers and preachers / Henry Fehren.
        p.   cm.
    ISBN 0-89390-271-3
    1. Catholic Church—Popular works. 2. Catholic
Church—History—1965- 3. Fehren, Henry. I. Title.
BX1754.F34 1993
282—dc20   93-30574

Printed in the United States of America

98 97 96 95 94 | 5 4 3 2 1

The chapters in this book, with the exception of "Lord of Mercy and Compassion," are a collection of articles originally published in U.S. Catholic *magazine.*

CONTENTS

PREFACE

What is this book about? It is about Jesus today.

But why *today*? "Jesus Christ is the same yesterday and today and forever" (Heb 13:8). In telling us to follow him, Jesus did not give us exact rules or a systematic path. We must learn how to follow him in the situation we, individually, are in today. Same Jesus, different times.

It would be convenient if he had left us a detailed map or a systematic way to follow him. Then this book, like a good Greek play, would have a beginning, a middle, and an end. But life is not that way. Nor can this book be.

Thus, after forty-five years of priestly, pastoral life, I write about various ways of relating to Jesus, of being one with him today. To be one with him, to live in unity with him, is not, of course, to be identical with him. God has made each of unique, different.

Mature Catholics, I emphasize, do not confuse the way, the truth, and the life of Jesus with man-made rules (yes, man-made — women, unfortunately, do not yet make rules in the church). As we are one with Jesus, we *are* the church.

ONE

A Matter of Conscience

Here is that word again. "The core of the book is the conscience of the warden." And again. "This is cinema of conscience."

Conscience.

Again and again I am seeing that word—not in church publications but in the secular press. "Group Loyalty vs. Individual Conscience" is the headline in one newspaper.

I was lately tromping around in the jungles of Borneo and Papua New Guinea and there, of all places, I was reading a Victorian novel, *The Warden*, by Anthony Trollope. The "warden" is not the head of a prison but is a Church of England functionary who receives a comfortable income as "warden" of a small home for twelve elderly men, a position in which he need do almost nothing.

"The core of the book is the conscience of the warden," says a critical essay accompanying the novel. The twelve destitute occupants of the almshouse are living a somewhat spartan life, yet a secure one; they are much better off here, for otherwise they could be homeless, hungry and on the streets.

The hospice had been founded and funded by the last will and testament of a man who had died many years ago. At the time of the story the occupants are receiving the same amount of benefit as when the will was made, but because of increased property values the endowment had increased tremendously. Yet only the warden received the increase.

The reverend warden is what we all would call a nice guy. Like us, he's a decent person, friendly, somewhat generous, plays the violoncello, does a conscientious job as a precentor at the cathedral, "in certain ways the best one can expect from human beings." Complacent, self-satisfied, undisturbed, at peace.

And then he read in the local newspaper: "On what foundation, moral or divine, traditional or legal, is grounded the warden's claim to the large income he receives from doing nothing?"

His conscience had begun to bother him before the newspaper attack, but the newspaper summed up his moral problems. From a slight twinge of conscience the ecclesiastic's moral perturbation grows until it becomes almost unbearable. "I cannot boast of my conscience," he says, "when it required the violence of a public newspaper to awaken it; but now that it is awake, I must obey it."

His bishop and the cathedral archdeacon give him cogent reasons for not giving up the unjust benefice, but he follows his conscience and gives it up and thus must henceforward lead a very frugal life. His decision, however, lacks perfection, for he is also motivated by a desire to escape the public attacks of the newspapers and others.

Trollope, as one critic points out, manages to capture the spirit of the mid-Victorian age: peace, quietude, equipoise, stability, compromise. Conscience is in remission; injustice is below one's gaze; morality is a surface placebo. It reminds me of the Reagan years.

So, having come back from the jungles of Borneo and Papua New Guinea, I read in the newspaper, "This is cinema of conscience." So I go to a movie about another jungle, the physical and moral jungle of Vietnam and the war, *Casualties of War*.

Five American soldiers are on patrol. The sergeant in command decides to kidnap and have them gangrape and eventually kill a young Vietnamese woman. Two of the group object, but one, with a rosary around his neck (which he takes off and puts in his pocket before he rapes the girl), gives in to peer pressure. The other is adamant; his conscience will not permit it. He also, at the risk of his life, reports the crime. The account is true and the objector now lives in anonymity.

Critics also say that the story is too simplistic: the good guy is too good and the bad guy too bad and we don't know how they got that way. The director saw the movie as a morality play, "a story not only of the corruption of the individual, but of society as well."

"It shows what happens," said the director, "when there seems to be no moral compass at all." A reviewer says that anything can be tolerated in a world devoid of moral values and no fixed norms by which behavior can be judged.

The horror of war can dislocate a person mentally, and we leave the ultimate judgment of any person to God. In Graham Greene's *The Lawless Roads*, an account of the Mexican government's persecution of the church, a man tells of a "whisky priest" who fled the isolated area. "But who can judge," the man asks, "what terror and hardship and isolation may have excused him in the eyes of God?"

When American soldiers at My Lai killed hundreds of innocent Vietnamese, including children, one killer said, "We carried out our orders, and I feel that we did not violate any moral standards." Another said, "Once you start, it's very easy to go on." A few soldiers refused the command to kill.

Why do decent people commit evil deeds? asks one reviewer. Just carrying out orders. Group loyalty. Fear. Peer pressure. Obedience to an "authority." Not getting involved. "The woman...gave me fruit from the tree, and I ate....The serpent tricked me..." (Gn 3:12-13).

The conscientious soldier in *Casualties* says, "Just because each one of us might at any second be blown away, everybody's acting like we can do anything and it don't matter what we do. But I'm thinking maybe it's all the other way around. The main thing is just the opposite, and because we might be dead in the next split second, we have to be extra careful about what we do—because maybe what we do matters more."

Yes, "mortals...die once, and after that the judgment" (Heb 9:27).

Since conscience is more than a morally unreliable instinct, it needs some formation. Many Catholics are confused about conscience today, for they were educated to believe that man-made church rules and regulations were the supreme law. They wonder why we can eat meat on Friday now and why it is not a sacrilege to drink water after midnight if they receive Holy Communion the next morning.

Two Catholic magazines have printed articles on conscience. In *Commonweal*, Fr. Bernard Häring, the great moral theologian, writes on "Building a Creative Conscience." "Building a creative conscience," he says, "means getting to know Jesus, and through him the meaning of love; it rescues us from mechanistic images of the conscience and immunizes us against fanatical legalism."

Graham Greene's delightful novel *Monsignor Quixote* reflects on the moral theology in which seminarians of my day were raised and which we on ordination unthinkingly handed on to the laity. A Spanish monsignor, made such by chance and ill-fitted to the breed, has discussions with a smalltown Communist mayor. The monsignor quotes, but questions, a real moral theologian, Fr. Heribert Jone, whom we in my day thought liberal compared to other moral theologians of the time but whose manual is a joke today.

We may say that this is history today, but many Catholics are still perplexed. John Gregory Dunne, raised Catholic, in his novel *The Red White and Blue* has a character say, "It was a mortal sin you saw a condemned movie. *Baby Doll*. That was condemned. You see that one? Then you committed a mortal sin, you saw *Baby Doll*. You couldn't get out of hell with a plenary indulgence, you know that?"

The other Catholic magazine with an article on conscience (and there may be others) is *Salt*, with an article on conscientious objection to war. I was glad to see it quote St. Thomas Aquinas:

> Anyone upon whom the ecclesiastical authority,
> in ignorance of true facts, imposes a demand
> that offends his clear conscience, should perish
> in excommunication rather than violate his
> conscience.

St. Peter puts it briefly: "We must obey God rather than any human authority" (Acts 5:29).

Having written thus far, I take a break and read today's *New York Times*. Sure enough, I see the words "On Our Conscience?" at the head of a column. The writer wonders whether the sin of racism is on the American conscience. Another columnist questions the morality or conscience of former President Bush and the Reverend Jesse Jackson. Both rightly condemn apartheid in South Africa. Yet the first African Mr. Bush invited to the White House and honored with a state visit is the cruel black dictator of Zaire, who has robbed his impoverished people of five billion dollars. Mr. Jackson visited a number of self-appointed black dictators in Africa but had not one word of criticism for their cruelty and greed.

It is good to see that the number of schools teaching business ethics has increased in the past ten years from three hundred to over three thousand.

Since "each of us will be accountable to God" (Rom 14:12), St. Paul commented frequently on conscience. "Therefore," he says, "I do my best always to have a clear conscience toward God and all people" (Acts 24:16). For him, love, which never harms the neighbor, is the fulfillment of the law (Rom 13:10).

Fr. Bernard Häring agrees with him:

> When we form our consciences primarily in response to the guiding laws of the Gospel and the Beatitudes, and devote ourselves unflaggingly to putting them into practice as best we can, we will continually make new discoveries, and they will be seen not as onerous or demanding but as invitations to growth.

Reflection Questions

- What feelings emerged as you read the story of the warden? Would you have been comfortable with his high pension for doing nothing? What about after the newspaper attacks? Was this all much ado about nothing?

- Have you ever had to choose between following orders and following your conscience? Did you pay a price for your decision?

- Under what circumstances would you go against your conscience?

- Is there a difference between "following your conscience" and "doing your own thing?" How do you distinguish between the two?

Two

The Packaging of Jesus

Magazines in the waiting room of doctors' and dentists' offices are always notoriously out of date by several months or even a year or more. The other day I had to take someone to a doctor's office. As we waited, as one always does, to be accepted into the inner office, I looked over, without much hope, the battered magazines lying around.

Among the newest ones was an old issue of *Harper's*, where I found an article called "He's Back!!!" It was about the Second Coming of Christ. Now why would that be in a secular magazine? *Harper's* is as likely to promote Jesus as I am to foster devotion to Our Lady of Necedah, Wisconsin.

The editor explains:

> One wonders how these professionals [public relations experts] would manage the Western world's most anticipated reappearance—the Second Coming of Jesus, as predicted in the Book of Revelation.

We've heard of "the making of the President," of how politicians these days hire media experts and public relations professionals to manage their election campaigns for them. The office seeker is told what clothes to wear, what topics to emphasize and what subjects to ignore. It's all in the image, how to make the best appeal to the voter.

Just as lawyers plan every word and gesture in the courtroom to influence the jurors, advertisers carefully calculate the best means of selling a political candidate, a car, a breakfast cereal or anything else. We are so aware of the power of the public relations experts today that in one election in New York and New Jersey there was more analysis of how the campaigns were managed than analysis of the competence of the campaigners to hold public office.

That is why, with tongue in cheek, *Harper's* called in six consultants to see how they would stage Christ's Second Coming "to win over American public opinion." Whether Jesus will need these pros is doubtful, for he said, "When the Son of Man comes in his glory, and all the angels with him, then he will sit on the throne of his glory. All the nations will be gathered before him..." (Mt 25:31-32).

Even though "all the tribes of the earth...will see 'the Son of Man coming on the clouds of heaven' with power and great glory" (Mt 24:30; Rv 1:7), the media mentors suggest a stint on a TV talk show, a comedy routine on "Saturday Night Live," a few modest miracles, properly religious fashion-designed clothing, speeches and attitudes to fit the various local mentalities on a nation-wide tour, a pro-homeless, anti-racist, one-minute television commercial, and a flashy new cover for the New Testament, including the words, "Billions Sold" and "Honk if You Love Jesus!"

I used to get irritated when salesmen would come to the rectory and say, "Well, Father, we're both salesmen. I'm selling aluminum siding (or whatever—lace surplices?) and you're selling religion." Perhaps they are right, in a way. We do try to present Jesus in such a way that people will become followers of him.

One way we "sell" Jesus is by sermons. Here, according to Anthony Trollope in his Victorian novel *Barchester Towers*, we often fail:

> There is, perhaps, no greater hardship at present inflicted on mankind in civilized times and free countries than the necessity of listening to sermons.
>
> No one but a preaching clergyman has, in these realms, the power of compelling an audience to sit silent and be tormented. No one but a preaching clergyman can revel in platitude, truisms and untruisms and yet receive, as his undisputed privilege, the same respectful demeanour as though words of impassioned eloquence, or persuasive logic, fell from his lips.
>
> Let a professor of law or physics find his place in a lecture-room and there pour forth jejune words and useless empty phrases, and he will pour them forth to empty benches. Let a barrister attempt to talk without talking well, and he will talk but seldom.
>
> A judge's charge need be listened to perforce by none but the jury, prisoner, and gaoler. A member of Parliament can be coughed down or counted out. Town-councilors can be tabooed.
>
> But no one can rid himself of the preaching clergyman. He is the bore of the age, the old man whom we Sindbads cannot shake off, the nightmare that disturbs our Sunday's rest, the incubus that overloads our religion and makes God's service distasteful.
>
> We are not forced into church! No: but we desire more than that. We desire not to be forced to stay away. We desire, nay, we are resolute, to enjoy the comfort of public worship, but we desire also that we may do so without an amount of tedium which ordinary human nature cannot endure with patience; that we may be able to leave the house of God

> without that anxious longing for escape which
> is the common consequence of common
> sermons.

It is a passage I should remember each time I ascend the pulpit. I like Trollope.

The best way, of course, to foster belief in Jesus is by one's own faith proven by saintliness.

At Christmas, when we commemorate Christ's coming two thousand years ago, we often speak also of his Second Coming, for which the first is a preparation. Those who would package Jesus for his Second Coming do not have an edge on Matthew and Luke in their presentation of his first coming. They do a brilliant job, for the infancy narratives are probably the best-known stories in the Western world. Century after century they are retold, presented in school plays, and exhibited in crib sets in homes and churches. Christmas is the most popular feast of the church year, and great artists have painted the nativity scene again and again.

From the annunciation to the presentation in the temple, it is a very appealing story. It has given birth to many other stories and to songs, hymns, plays, poems, even an opera. Many of them we deem sentimental, but sentiment comes from our humanity. Still, I dread the day that we'll hear at the Christmas liturgy, "Happy birthday to you, happy birthday to you, happy birthday, Baby Jesus, happy birthday to you."

Matthew and Luke were not present at Christ's birth, but their accounts have poetic beauty, emotional appeal and human interest. They were not trying to write cute stories and they knew that they were not writing detailed history. The gospels were written long after Jesus had left this earth. Mark and John ignored Christ's infancy but Matthew and Luke wanted to tell more about who Jesus is and about his mission.

Mark, usually considered the oldest of the gospels, begins with the baptism of Jesus. For him, according to Fr. Raymond Brown, that is where God reveals who Jesus is. For Matthew, God does this at the conception and birth of Jesus.

Matthew especially uses Old Testament imagery, but he and Luke create a beautiful, heart-warming, touching Christmas story, an account in which every line is significant, full of meaning, theological, filled with God's revelation. We cannot let the glitz and busyness and business of the "holiday season" weaken, distort or destroy what God has to tell us in the infancy narratives about our Savior.

"Mary treasured all these words and pondered them in her heart" (Lk 2:19). If she did it, it must be good for us to do so—or we will be the losers.

"Packaging" may be a crude, modern advertiser's term for Matthew's and Luke's compositions of the infancy narrative, the purpose of which is to present Jesus as the savior. But what a brilliant job they do! We have expectancy: there are two annunciations: one to Mary (well known) and one to Joseph (often forgotten; Mt 1:20). There is suspense: the escape of the child Jesus from the wicked King Herod. Rejection, which we have all experienced: no room in the inn. A teenager helping an old person: Mary going in haste to help the aged Elizabeth.

An aging woman told me that the golden years are not so golden. But in the infancy depiction there is hope for the elderly. Elizabeth and Zechariah have a famous baby in their old age, and in the temple at the presentation is 84-year-old Anna, who "began to praise God and to speak about the child to all who were looking for the redemption of Jerusalem" (Lk 2:38)—a liberation theologian.

Widows may take note that she is a widow, and Simeon gives us the best night prayer of all time. And we have the lovely offering of a pair of turtle doves, the offering of the poor. (And a coo for bird lovers.)

This "preferential option for the poor," heard so often today, is also seen in the poor, coarse shepherds to whom is made the first announcement, from heaven, of the saving event which can save humankind and alter the course of history.

And we have the satisfaction of seeing that it is the affluent magi (in later folklore transformed into kings) who must come looking for the poor child and offer exotic, rich gifts. We have a husband agreeing with his wife: "His name is John" (Lk 1:63); consolation: Simeon now ready to die happily; fear: "What then will this child become?" (Lk 1:66); curiosity: the shepherds; humility coupled with justice: Mary's Magnificat; a possible sex scandal: Mary pregnant without her espoused's participation; a lesson for adolescents: John "grew and became strong in spirit" (Lk 1:80) and Jesus "increased in wisdom and in years, and in divine and human favor" (Lk 2:52) and was *obedient* to Mary and Joseph. Intrigue: Herod and the magi. Thrills: the escape to Egypt. Prophecy: "This child is destined for the falling and the rising of many in Israel..." (Lk 2:34).

The genius of Matthew and Luke gives us the reality of Christmas. Unbelievers today may try to turn it into plastic and tinsel and Santa Claus, but with Elizabeth's neighbors and relatives (Lk 1:58) we happily accept the angel's call to rejoice (Lk 1:28), for Christmas is here again.

Reflection Questions

- Imagine Jesus on a talk show. Would this even be possible? If he appeared on a talk show, how would he compare to other guests? Or would he be host?

- Have you ever complained about a sermon? When you did, were you asking for better packaging or something else? What?

- If you were given the task of "selling" Jesus to the world—without changing his message—how would you do it? Talk shows? Bumper stickers? TV ads? Preaching?

- Fr. Fehren said he dreads the day when someone sings "Happy Birthday" to Jesus at a Christmas liturgy. Do you agree? Why or why not?

- How do liturgy, Scripture, and the church year compare to modern ways of selling a concept or a product? Do you think the church needs to update itself or go back to some traditional values?

- What or who "sold you" on Catholicism or Christianity? Was the process different than the way you might have been sold on a new car or a political candidate? If so, how?

THREE

Be There With

Once upon a time, according to a Sufi story recalled by Fr. Henry Nouwen, there was a man who traveled to a strange land. Here he saw people fleeing in terror from a wheatfield. They were wheat growers and had been harvesting. When he sought an explanation they said that there was a monster in the field.

He went to the field and found only a watermelon, the "monster." Intending to be kind, he offered to kill the "monster" for them. He hacked the melon off its vine and then cut a slice and began to eat it. The people then become even more terrified of him. "He will eat us also," they cried and then drove him off with their pitchforks.

Another traveler to the same country found himself in a similar situation: people in terror of a monster in their wheatfield. Instead of offering to kill the monster, he said that it must be dangerous and he tiptoed away from it. Thus he gained their confidence; he spent some time with them and gradually taught them some elementary horticultural facts. They lost their fear of the melon and even began to cultivate watermelons.

The first traveler was a good man but he merely pitied the wheat growers; the second entered into their fears, suffered with them — he had compassion.

There is another story, told by a Jesuit missionary in the Brazilian jungle. A monkey, for his first time, saw

14

a fish in a river. "Oh, the poor fish," he said. "It will drown." His heart was moved to pity. So he picked the fish out of the water to give it air (and life, as he thought). The only life the monkey knew, of course, was life outside of water. After flopping around for a little while on dry land, the fish died. The monkey was sad to see that, but he consoled himself, "At least it died on this nice land and not in that cold water."

We find the word "love" all over the New Testament. It is the supreme law, says Jesus, quoting the Old Testament. "For the whole law," says St. Paul, "is summed up in a single commandment, 'You shall love your neighbor as yourself'" (Gal 5:14). That love must extend to compassion. "Be merciful," Jesus tells us, "just as your Father is merciful" (Lk 6:36).

Here is a true account, not a story; it happened recently. A poor woman holding a baby was begging outside a church. A rich woman, entering to pray, saw her and gave her a ten dollar bill. As the donor went into the church she noticed that the beggar also did. The beggar stuffed the ten dollars into the Poor Box.

"Look at that! She put it in the Poor Box!" exclaimed the giver indignantly. "It's the last time I would give her something. Why didn't she feed her baby with that ten?" The rich woman (I can testify that she is) had a spark of generosity and a touch of love for a stranger, but she lacked compassion. She failed to *be* with that poor woman. Maybe the poor woman had provisions for the child and now wanted to share this gift with other poor people.

She had compassion, but the rich one failed to understand the ways of Jesus, who praised the impractical widow for giving her mite in the temple (Mk 12:42). The rich one was not inclined to understand the motives of the poor one. The point at issue is not riches and poverty but to suffer with someone else.

To have compassion means to suffer with someone else, out of love. It does not mean that we identify with that person; that is impossible, for, as an old rabbi remarked, God does not do the same thing twice. Each person God creates is different from any other. In our compassion we cannot substitute ourselves for the suffering person. We cannot take upon ourselves their suffering. In spite of all our efforts, they will still suffer.

Jesus bore our sins upon the cross (Heb 9:28; 1 Pt 2:24), though we are still sinners. We know Jesus as a person who suffered, and millions of Christians have found their sufferings not removed but alleviated by the presence of Christ. His compassion compels his presence and we are able to accept our suffering with a peaceful heart because of his compassion.

Though St. Paul tells us that because we are God's chosen race we should clothe ourselves in compassion (Col 3:12), we may hesitate to be compassionate to someone who is a sinner. Christ did not seem to have a problem with compassion to sinners. He tells with approval, after Samaritans had rejected him (Lk 9:53), the story of a Samaritan traveler who was moved with compassion when he saw a man who had fallen "into the hands of robbers." After a priest and a Levite had ignored the stranger, who had been robbed and injured, the Samaritan tenderly took care of him and provided for him. "Which of these three, do you think," Jesus asks the lawyer who had asked him about achieving eternal life, "was a neighbor to the man who fell into the hands of the robbers?" The reply: "The one who showed him mercy." Jesus' response: "Go and do likewise" (Lk 10:30-37).

Some people who are not willing to go and do likewise are a majority of 192 physicians, dentists, chiropractors and mental health specialists in one California county. They were not willing to treat patients with AIDS or who were HIV positive. No compassion there.

Likewise with the city council of an Illinois municipality. A man of compassion wanted to open a hospice for people with AIDS. A professional home care specialist, he was fully qualified and his work, full-time, would be donated. The city council voted against it. The case was taken to court, and the judge, finding the council's reasons irrational and stupid, overruled the council.

People usually do not want pity; they sense a loss of dignity in being a pitiable creature. "Blessed are the merciful" (Mt 5:7), but we must be careful that we do not act superior in showing mercy to others. In compassion we do not sit in judgment; we accept the humanity of the person and we know that the person is different. God is too creative to go in for clones.

In being compassionate we try to understand another person, "where they come from, where they are at the moment." Jesus gives examples of this when he defends the disciples for pulling off the heads of grain and eating them on the Sabbath and when he then heals the man with a shriveled hand on the Sabbath. He explains that compassion is more important than the law (Mt 12:1-13).

God didn't just look down on us from heaven and extend a hand. He became one of us.

> [He] emptied himself,
>> taking the form of a slave,
>> being born in human likeness.
> And being found in human form,
>> he humbled himself
>> and became obedient to the point of death —
>> even death on a cross (Phil 2:7-8).

That's compassion.

Even to those in whom we are not interested or even to those who hate us we show compassion. It is more than turning the other cheek. It is even more than "pray for those who persecute you."

God the Son, enjoying eternal bliss in heaven, did not when he saw our miseries on earth say, "I'll pray for you to my Father." He came to share our suffering.

When I hear someone say, "I'll remember you in my prayers," I feel like saying, "Come, pour wine and oil into my wounds, as the Samaritan did. Any pay for the care, as the Samaritan did. And don't just give me advice; come and do what needs to be done."

Yes, we need the prayers of others, and Jesus did pray for us, but often "I'll pray for you" can be a pious copout. It costs nothing and can be an easy sop to the conscience and an avoidance of true compassion. The English poet William Blake (d. 1827) in his poem "Jerusalem" says, "He who would do good to another, must do it in minute particulars. / General good is the plea of the scoundrel, hypocrite, and flatterer."

Whoever wrote the epistle to the Hebrews commended people he knew who had "compassion for those who were in prison," and he later urges, "Remember those who are in prison, as though you were in prison with them" (10:34; 13:3).

"Rejoice with those who rejoice," says St. Paul, "weep with those who weep" (Rom 12:15). At least put up with them, according to an old story from The Talmud: An aged man, whom Abraham hospitably invited to his tent, refused to join him in prayer to the one spiritual God. Learning that he was a fire-worshiper, Abraham drove him from his door. That night God appeared to Abraham in a vision and said, "I have borne with that ignorant man for seventy years; could you not have patiently suffered him for one night?"

Writing on the humanity of Jesus, Monika Hellwig, theologian, says that as Jesus was the Word of God, the image of God and the wisdom of God, he also was the divine compassion made visible. To be with Jesus is to be compassionate.

So before I put Blake back on the bookshelf, let's look at another poem of his, "On Another's Sorrow":

> Can I see another's woe,
> And not be in sorrow too?

Can I see another's grief,
And not seek for kind relief?

Can I see a falling tear,
And not feel my sorrow's share?
Can a father see his child
Weep, nor be with sorrow filled?

Can a mother sit and hear
An infant groan, an infant fear?
No, no! never can it be!
Never, never can it be!

And can He who smiles on all
Hear the wren with sorrows small,
Hear the small bird's grief and care,
Hear the woes that infants bear—

And not sit beside the nest,
Pouring pity in their breast,
And not sit the cradle near,
Weeping tear on infant's tear?

And not sit both night and day,
Wiping all our tears away?
Oh no! never can it be!
Never, never can it be!

He doth give His joy to all:
He becomes an infant small,
He becomes a man of woe,
He doth feel the sorrow too.

Think not thou canst sigh a sigh,
And thy Maker is not by:
Think not thou canst weep a tear,
And thy Maker is not near.

Oh, He gives us to His joy.
That our grief He may destroy:

Till our grief is fled and gone
He doth sit by us and moan.

Reflection Questions

- Have their been instances in your life when you have seen someone—perhaps yourself—hurt another person by trying to help him or her? Did this happen because the person did not understand the other person, or for some other reason?

- Have you ever given money to someone in need, only to be annoyed at what they did with the money? Would Fr. Fehren's admonition that the giver failed to "be with" apply in this instance?

- Are there limits to compassion as Fr. Fehren has defined it? Are there people even Jesus could not "suffer with?" For example, Hitler, a child molester, an arsonist? Or would Jesus find a way to "be with" them? Is there a call for us to do the same?

FOUR

A Letter from Mary

"I just wish that my clients would try a little to know God and they could be as happy as I am. I have had all of the best the world has to offer."

Those two sentences are from a newsy letter I received a week ago. Before I could continue reading, I had to read those lines again and again. They were not the main point of the letter; they were only an added commentary on an event she had just written about.

The writer's name is Mary, and I immediately thought about another Mary who said,

> My soul magnifies the Lord,
>   and my spirit rejoices in God my savior....
> for the Mighty One has done great things for me,
>   and holy is his name" (Lk 1:47,49).

I began to consider what the present Mary had to be happy about when I began to wonder what Mary of Nazareth had to be happy about. Yes, all ages to come would call her blessed, as she said, but that would happen only a few centuries after her death.

Most women are joyful when they are about to become mothers, and Mary was no exception. And she could be happy that her son would be great with dignity, called Son of the Most High, be given the throne of David and rule over the house of Jacob forever (Lk

1:32-33). I presume that she enjoyed her visit to Elizabeth (while poor lonely Joseph suffered his own cooking for three months).

But after that?

Jesus had no throne, he didn't rule, and no one called him "Son of the Most High." A big crowd did welcome him to Jerusalem and call him a prophet (Mt 21:8-11) and at other times crowds came to listen and to be healed. Mary could be happy about that. Pilate was the only one to label him a king, but that was in mockery of the Jews.

One strain of Catholic piety saw Mary not as the Joyful Mother, as she proclaimed herself in the Magnificat, but as the Sorrowful Mother or the Mother of Sorrows. This devotion lists her sorrows as seven, and, indeed, on reading the gospels we are probably more aware of her sufferings than of her joys.

The Good News, the gospels, sometimes seems like bad news. Certainly Mary, after the good news of the annunciation, had plenty of bad news. Biblical scholars are again emphasizing the humanity of Jesus. If we are to fully relate to him and see him as one of us, as our brother, as one who is like us in all things except sin, who was "born in human likeness" (Phil 2:7), we must know him not only as God but as a fully human being.

The letter to the Hebrews emphasizes this:

> Since, therefore, the children share flesh and
> blood, he himself likewise shared the same
> things....For it is clear that he did not come to
> help angels, but the descendants of Abraham.
> Therefore he had to become like his brothers
> and sisters in every respect, so that he might
> be a merciful and faithful high priest in the
> service of God....Because he himself was
> tested by what he suffered, he is able to help
> those who are being tested (2:14-18).

> For we do not have a high priest who is
> unable to sympathize with our weaknesses,
> but we have one who in every respect has
> been tested as we are, yet without sin (4:15).

It is helpful to our faith if we see Mary and other holy ones in the Bible as people, human beings who could fear and suffer and be happy, who because of their faith could have joy even in their suffering.

At the annunciation the angel told Mary not to fear, but anxiety soon followed. She was pregnant but not through Joseph, and he suspected her of adultery. The Law (Dt 22:20-21) would have her stoned to death, but Joseph decided to divorce her quietly (Mt 1:19). The angel cleared that up for him.

Usually listed as the first of Mary's sorrows is Simeon's prophecy when Jesus was presented in the temple. "A sword will pierce your own soul" (Lk 2:35) he told Mary. Although popular piety sees this prediction as anticipation or foreknowledge on Mary's part of future sorrows, the text is obscure. One Scripture scholar says that Mary, too, had to learn (Mary, when the shepherds left, "treasured all these words and pondered them in her heart" [Lk 2:19]) and that this learning process "is not without its perils and its suffering."

Mary and Joseph were poor, for they gave the offering of the poor, "a pair of turtledoves or two young pigeons" (Lk 2:24), rather than a year-old lamb.

Mary was probably excited by the visit of the magi, but that led to her second sorrow, the flight into Egypt to protect the life of Jesus. There are millions of refugees in the world today; Mary and Joseph also had the experience of fleeing to a foreign country. They had to leave suddenly, at night, for Herod was "about to search for the child, to destroy him" (Mt 2:13).

It must have been painful to hear of the massacre of "all the children in and around Bethlehem who were two years old or under" (Mt 2:16). Even after the death of Herod, Mary and Joseph had to move to a new place and live in fear because Archelaus had succeeded his father as king; he was another monster.

One of the greatest agonies for parents is to suffer the disappearance of a child. After a day's journey on their way back from Jerusalem, where they had gone for the Passover, Mary and Joseph realized that the boy Jesus was with neither of them. He was alone in the city. So back they went in great anxiety to look for him. On the third day they found him in the temple.

"Look, your father and I have been searching for you in great anxiety" (Lk 2:48) Mary told him. Although he would go back with Mary and Joseph and be obedient to them, he distanced himself from them by saying that he had to be in his Father's house. They did not understand.

The four final sorrows have to do with Christ's suffering and death: meeting Jesus as he carried his cross on the way to Calvary (not in the gospels) and his being pierced with a lance and being taken down from the cross. The death of an only child is grief enough for a widowed mother, but the conditions of Christ's death would seem to bring sorrow to the breaking point.

Jesus, a good and innocent man who loved and taught and healed, was condemned to a public and shameful death. Mary was present at the crucifixion, saw the thorns on his head, saw his bloody body, heard the crowds jeer at him, endured his long agony. She saw the ugliness and brutality and heard Christ's desolate cry, "My God, my God, why have you forsaken me?" (Mt 27:46). What a test of her faith!

Every torture inflicted on the body of Jesus, said St. Jerome, was a wound in the heart of his mother. Finally Jesus died and the body was taken down from the cross. We presume that Mary then washed that body, which she had washed when Jesus was a child. At last the satisfaction of doing something. She was helpless while he was on the cross.

"Near the cross of Jesus were his mother..." (Jn 19:25). She was there through it all and then the body was carried to a nearby, dark, borrowed tomb. Joseph of Arimathea then "rolled a great stone to the door of the tomb and went away" (Mt 27:60).

And Mary was left to reflect on the angel's words to her many years ago: "Greetings, favored one! The Lord is with you" (Lk 1:28). What would our reaction be, had we to suffer such a profound sorrow? Would we rejoice? Would we consider ourselves blessed?

I thought of these questions as I read the letter of the other Mary. She rejoices in God her Savior. She has led a life of poverty. Her husband died at age forty-six, leaving her with eight children. The first child was born mentally retarded. Mary has taken care of him at home all his lifetime. Another son died at age twenty-two. Another son has severe mental problems and has fathered six children by three women. And, as many a Catholic parent has today, she has suffered the loss of faith in some of her children.

She is seventy-eight years old, yet she spends her time taking care of other elderly people. In her little tin car she picks them up and takes them to doctor and dentist appointments. She goes to their homes to visit and listen to them. She has no garage, so in winter her car freezes up. Somehow she gets it started. If there is a heavy snowfall, she shovels a way to the street.

A close friend of Dorothy Day until Dorothy died, she dresses simply and is free of avarice. She loves her "clients," as she calls them, even if they are weepy, cross, ailing or barely still "with it" mentally. She just wishes that they knew God as she does and could thus be joyful.

In chapter eleven of 2 Corinthians, St. Paul lists the many, many sufferings he has undergone: being beaten, stoned, shipwrecked, imprisoned; undergone hardships, sleepless nights, hunger, thirst, cold, and danger—to mention only some. Yet he says that he is content with his suffering (12:10). If his blood has to be shed, he writes from prison, "I am glad and rejoice with all of you" (Phil 2:17). Jesus tells us to be glad and rejoice when we are insulted and persecuted (Mt 5:11-12).

Again and again we find in the New Testament this theme of joy in suffering. "You cheerfully accepted the plundering of your possessions" (Heb 10:34). "Rejoice insofar as you are sharing Christ's sufferings," advises St. Peter (1 Pt 4:13).

I was surprised that a musical has been made about Archbishop Romero of El Salvador, who was martyred with the financial help of our government. A musical made about the assassination of this holy man? It didn't seem right. Yet it is fitting, said Fr. Jon Sobrino, a Jesuit theologian from El Salvador who by chance missed being killed when six of his fellow Jesuits and their housekeeper and her child were butchered. "Martyrdom must be celebrated. The most joyful Masses in El Salvador have been to celebrate those who have been assassinated." Indeed, throughout the centuries, we have been celebrating the feasts of the martyrs.

None of us can avoid suffering, but we can be joyful about it only if the words of Elizabeth to Mary can be applied to us: "Blessed is she who believed that there would be a fulfillment of what was spoken to her by the Lord" (Lk 1:45). Faith.

Reflection Questions

- Is Mary principally a figure of joy or a figure of sorrow for you?

- Do the sorrows of Mary seem especially extraordinary or do they seem to be something that any mother (or parent) could identify with?

- Do you identify with any of the "sorrows" in Mary's life?

- Is Mary's life a source of comfort to you, or is her life irrelevant to yours?

FIVE

Hands On

Want to receive the greatest invitation you could ever receive? From the most important person who could invite you? Yes, a personal invitation, an invitation from Jesus. Here it is:

"Come, you that are blessed by my Father, inherit the kingdom prepared for you from the foundation of the world" (Mt 25:34).

A kingdom prepared for me! But, as we know, there is no such thing as a free lunch. Yes, there is a hitch. Invitations are addressed to selected people—in this case to people who show their acceptance of Jesus by doing what we call the corporal works of mercy: giving food and drink to the hungry and thirsty, welcoming strangers, clothing the naked and visiting the sick and imprisoned.

This scene in Matthew (25:31-46) is often called the Last Judgment, but it is not an invitation given as we take our last breath. It is an invitation given now to those who follow Jesus' way of love.

It is not enough to cry out, "Lord, Lord" (Mt 7:21). So as a for-instance, let's take visiting the sick. "I was sick and you took care of me" (Mt 25:36).

In one way, Jesus doesn't get much chance to go visit the sick, for before he can go to them they are brought to him in droves (Mk 6:56; Lk 4:40). He does tell the centurion that he will come to his home and heal his serving boy (Mt 8:7); however, when his dear friends Mary and Martha send word that their brother Lazarus is ill, he delays visiting them until Lazarus is dead. This would seem cruelty on his part, but he does it, he says, "for God's glory" (Jn 11:4), and then he raises Lazarus from the dead.

The words of Isaiah the prophet are applied to Jesus: "He took our infirmities and bore our diseases" (Mt 8:17). He "went throughout Galilee" and he "went about all the cities...curing every disease and every sickness" (Mt 4:23; 9:35). Reading the gospels, we see that the only thing more important to him than curing bodily ailments was teaching, and that was a means to curing spiritual illness.

Medical care was primitive at the time, and physical sickness was usually associated with sin. Jesus tells the apostles to "cure the sick, raise the dead, cleanse the lepers, cast out demons" (Mt 10:8). And, says Mark, they "anointed with oil many who were sick and cured them" (6:13). Anointing them with oil means that they placed their hands on them, which is what Jesus does, as we see again and again in the gospels. The care is personal. Jesus "stretched out his hand and touched" the leper (Mt 8:3).

Touched the leper. Beautiful words—and necessary if we are truly to "visit the sick." One bishop sanctimoniously and with due publicity visits people with AIDS and even touches them but then in public proclamations condemns them to eternal hellfire.

Jesus didn't discriminate. He loved all the sick and he put his hands on them. I have not seen that in the 110 days this past year, several hours a day, that I have spent visiting a sick person—Juan, to give him a name—in a hospital run by nuns. I am not sitting in judgment of the nuns, for I believe that finding competent, caring help is extremely difficult. All the nuns are in administration at the hospital; not one is a nurse.

Just out of nostalgia I would like to see one sister nursing patients, stretching out her hand as Jesus did to touch patients. The nurses, orderlies and whatever at this place are abrupt, impersonal, indifferent. The patient is treated as a thing rather than as a person. Perhaps the staff is tired of seeing sick people five days a week.

For them it's a paying job, not a work of mercy. Juan's eye doctor is very brusque, says nothing helpful, never calls him by name, and charges $210 for a brief stop. Juan's regular doctor has walked by his room without looking in. "I was sick and you visited me." No.

Juan is an alien and has no family here to visit him. He is almost totally blind, so he cannot read or watch TV. He is attached to a heavy IV machine, so he is not very mobile. Thus he needs visitors to help pass the long hours. A few friends have been most helpful. I have tried to get others to visit or telephone him but most are busy with work and their families.

When he is not in the hospital, I take him to my home and care for him here. It's no big deal, because for reasons of celibacy I have no wife or children to be concerned about. A visiting nurse stops in three times a week and treats him like a person, not a case. "I was sick and you visited me." Yes.

"Why do you do it?" people ask. "You have no obligation." Because God put him there in my path and I could not, like the priest and the Levite, pass to the other side of the street (Lk 10:25-37). We note in this account how the Samaritan personally dressed the wounds of the injured man and persevered in his care. Jesus said, "Go and do likewise" (Lk 10:37), and I thought that for once I would.

Besides, I haven't been a patient in a hospital for fifty years; I thought I had better show some gratitude to God. And I do not want to hear Jesus say to me, "I was sick and you did not visit me. Out of my sight, you condemned, into that everlasting fire prepared for the devil and his angels!" Juan is forty-three, weighs ninety-eight, and is dying of AIDS.

I know of countless numbers of people who at great sacrifice are taking care of sick persons in the manner of Jesus. One woman takes care of seven children in her home; their ages range from a few months to eight years. All have AIDS. When one dies she suffers greatly but she takes in another. A Benedictine Brother with a PhD in English from Oxford rented a house and made it a hospice for people with AIDS. He lives with them. When the owner put the house up for sale, the abbey bought it.

AIDS is a terrible affliction not only because the person knows that death is inevitable in a year or two or three in the prime of life but also because of the opprobrium attached to it. Even HIV-positive people, before the full onset of AIDS, have been fired from jobs, evicted from homes, denied health insurance and been refused medical and dental care.

One young man with AIDS went home to die and his family were glad to have him, but this was in the Bible Belt and the town, including the mayor, turned against him. The townspeople (I saw this on a TV talk show) were stupid and vicious. They forgot one line from their Bible.

Sometimes in newspaper obituaries families disguise the cause of death because they are ashamed that a family member died of AIDS.

Care of the sick has been a mark of the church since its inception. When John in prison wanted to know if Jesus was the messiah, Jesus indicated that healing would be a mark of his kingdom: "the blind receive their sight, the lame walk, the lepers are cleansed, the deaf hear" (Mt 11:5). He then sent the apostles out "to proclaim the kingdom of God and to heal" (Lk 9:2), which they did—and Christ's followers have been doing so ever since.

The wealthy Fabiola turned her country home into a refuge for the sick poor and took care of them herself. St. Basil and St. Gregory Nazianzen, both bishops, tended the sick with their own hands. St. John Chrysostom spent all the money he could find on building hospitals. Charlemagne ordered that every monastery and cathedral have a hospital. Many religious orders, societies and confraternities had as their chief aim the care of the sick.

St. Francis of Assisi said, "In the sick you see the infirmities which Jesus took upon himself for our sakes." For a while he lived at the leper house at Gubbio, where he washed the feet of the lepers, treated their sores, and even kissed them. St. Clare was just as devoted to the sick. St. Elizabeth brought the sick into her castle and personally took care of them.

St. Catherine of Siena, who had spent years taking care of the sick, was noted for taking care of the ailing whom no one else wanted even when the Black Death littered the streets with corpses. St. Vincent de Paul enjoined the Sisters of Charity to treat the ill with the compassion of Christ. The list of holy people who have hands-on treatment to the sick is endless. We'll conclude with St. Camillus de Lellis, who, though an invalid, for forty-six years would even crawl on hands and knees to assist the ailing.

There is no shortage of examples to inspire us in our care of the sick. Because the sick are usually confined they are not visible—out of sight, out of mind. Today because medical science can prolong the lives of even those most seriously ill, we may have more and more on the sick list, people needing our attention, people whom in one way or the other we ought to "visit."

This brings on many moral problems. Should we spend thousand upon thousands of dollars keeping a moribund person "alive" in a state of vegetation while a baby next door is dying of malnutrition because of poverty? Or keeping "alive" at the same cost a pre-

mature three-pound baby that will be beaten and probably killed by its cocaine parents? The few people I
know opposed to "mercy killing" are more opposed to
mercy than to killing.

If our life is a gift from God, it is something that we
own, the only thing that we really own. Why cannot we
then terminate it if we wish? It seems that some of the
early martyrs practically committed suicide, a death
they could in faith have avoided, had they not so
zealously wished to be with Jesus in heaven. Jesus
could have avoided his own death (Mt 26:53). Was his
death a "mercy killing?" He allowed himself to be killed
because he had mercy on us.

Be wary of using the fifth commandment pro or con
"life"; the Hebrews slaughtered men, women and children to conquer the "holy land." Just read the Jewish
Bible, the Old Testament.

I used to think of the Knights of Malta (where Bush
and Gorbachev met) as a group of rich, male Catholics
with silly titles and headgear, but their original purpose
was the care of the sick and the weak; we are doing just
that, says the new Grand Master.

Up until the ninth century, lay people, not just
priests, could anoint the sick. There are many, many
ways of "visiting the sick." I have learned that to visit
the sick is to suffer. But if we do it in the hands-on
manner of Jesus, as Tobiah put fish gall on the eyes of
his father and peeled away the cataracts (Tb 11:9-13),
we will hear the voice of Jesus saying, "Come, inherit
the kingdom prepared for you from the foundation of
the world."

Reflection Questions

- Do you have memories of visiting the sick or of
  providing some other "hands on" care such as Fr.

Fehren provided to Juan? How did you feel during those times?

- What makes the difference between the "hands off" care provided by Juan's regular doctor and the "hands on" care of the visiting nurse? Is it touch? Is it attention? Is it time? What did it mean to treat a Juan as a "person?"

- Have you ever been seriously ill? What role did medical personnel play in your recovery? What role did visitors play?

- Can you think of people who provide "hands on" care? Who are they? What is their profession? What are your feelings about them?

- What are your feelings about Fr. Fehren's comment: "The few people I know who are opposed to mercy killing are more opposed to mercy than to killing."

SIX

Where Were You?

As I rode a New York City subway train to Columbia University on the upper west side of Manhattan, I was delighted to see that the 86th Street station had been refurbished. The walls had been re-tiled and ceramic works of art had been embedded into the walls. The station was bright, clean, new.

Because of the old age of this huge system, many of the 468 stations are dingy and most were made worse in appearance by the graffiti slobbered all over them by mentally deficient hoodlums. All 6,300 cars had been cleaned of graffiti and many new cars were on the tracks. Most stations, however, were still a mess, so it was a relief to see the 86th Street station looking so great. It was an oasis for weary subway riders.

But then—oh, no! oh, yes!—someone with a destructive, ugly mind, someone with a contempt for God and God's creation, had smeared the walls from one end of the station to the other with streaks of paint. Yes, a small incident, when we consider the global effort to destroy our planet. It isn't Chernobyl; it's just the 86th Street station. It isn't industrial pollution of our soil, rivers, lakes, the ocean, and even the atmosphere itself. It was just a perverse, evil mind doing what it could do to desecrate God's creation.

The despoiler did not hear Isaiah's question:

> Who has measured the waters in the hollow of
>   his hand
> and marked off the heavens with a span,
> enclosed the dust of the earth in a measure,
>   and weighed the mountains in scales
>   and the hills in a balance?
> Have you not known? Have you not heard?
> The LORD is the everlasting God,
>   the Creator of the ends of the earth (40:12,28).

Can you forget, Isaiah again asks, "the LORD, your Maker, who stretched out the heavens and laid the foundations of the earth"? (51:13) When we throw trash on the sidewalk, when we toss cans out the car window, when we are unconcerned about the things we use at home that cannot be recycled, when we invest in or buy stock in industries that pollute God's good earth, we are forgetting.

I hope that it is just forgetting, for we are really showing disdain for God's goodness and we are being ungrateful for what he graciously has given us.

We begin the Apostle's Creed, "I believe in God, the Father Almighty, Creator of heaven and earth." We begin the Nicene Creed, usually said at Mass, "We believe in one God, the Father, the Almighty, maker of heaven and earth, of all that is seen and unseen." Perhaps we should ask if belief in God as creator has any effect on us. What does it mean for us? If faith is the living of our belief, how do we manifest faith in God as creator?

The story of creation in the book of Genesis is awesome, beautiful and poetic. It is a story of God's love for us. "God saw everything that he had made, and indeed, it was very good" (Gn 1:31). If God found it good, we also must find it good.

I was surprised at the number of pages (sixteen) devoted to creation in Fr. Karl Rahner's *Encyclopedia of Theology*. "God's creative action," says theologian

Pieter Smulder, "is not simply a thing of the past, it takes place here and now and is yet to come....Creation is an act of the present instant" (p. 312).

Creation, according to another theologian, is a spontaneous act which can have no other source or cause but the initiative of love. "Creation is pure generosity, the act of loving and giving" (p. 319). It is a mistake to take God's love for granted and not respond to it. God does not need creation; since it is a sign of God's love for us, we should be ashamed to destroy or even to deface it.

I recall a cartoon of a cave-age woman pointing to the sky and saying to her husband who was sitting at the edge of the cave, "Look, there's that big ball up there again." Each day she was astonished to find the sun up there again. I am too. I am constantly amazed at the created world, astounded that it is there—its size, its complexity and intricacy, its beauty. I feel like a beggar walking through Tiffany's jewelry store.

It's impossible that it be there, and yet it is. God in his generosity gave it to me for my use for a number of years. It is all sacred, for God made it all. Thus I must treat it with care and respect. Those are God's orders: "The LORD God took the man and put him in the garden of Eden to till it and keep it" (Gn 2:15).

In his *Holy Rule* for monks, St. Benedict (d. 547), writing about the cellarer, says, "Let him look upon all the vessels of the monastery as though they were the consecrated vessels of the altar." Even earlier, St. Basil (d. 379) wrote about the "consecrated" character of all things to be used by monks; he says that misuse of them is a sacrilege.

Cassian (d. 435) goes to the extreme, but we get the point:

> If anything whatever has once been brought into
> the monastery, the brethren claim that it must
> be treated with utmost reverence as a holy

> thing...even in the case of things which are
> considered as common and paltry, so that if
> they change the position of these things, and
> put them in a better place, or if they fill a bottle
> with water, or if they remove a little dust from
> the oratory or from their cell, they believe with
> implicit faith that they will receive a reward from
> the Lord.

Every hair on a person' head has been counted by God, says Jesus. God sees everything. Not even a sparrow can fall from the sky without the Father knowing (Mt 10:29-30). As a child I aimed a slingshot at sparrows; God saw to it that I always missed. Later I stupidly hunted pheasants, ducks and partridge. I always missed. Thank you, God.

These beautiful birds, which God created ("Let birds fly above the earth across the dome of the sky. So God created...every winged bird of every kind. And God saw that it was good. God blessed them..." [Gn 1:20-22]) are now killed by people not for food but for "sport." A *New York Times* article about hunting Canada geese talks only about guns, steel shot, equipment, shells and the "auto loader." "I fired at a bird. It fell. I picked another one, and fired again. It fell. One bird was within range. I bagged it with my third shot."

As with the sparrow, God saw the geese fall from the sky. And the "hunter," insecure about his own masculinity, proved that he was macho by destroying these good, innocent beautiful witnesses to God's love for us.

We sing in Psalm 104:10,12:

> You make springs gush forth in the valleys....
> By the streams the birds of the air have their
>   habitation;
>   they sing among the branches

—unless the hunters with their killer guns find them and murder beauty which God created for all of us. The

38

age of the caveman is over; since we don't have sabre-toothed tigers to hunt, it is ridiculous to substitute these sleek, delicate creatures of the air.

I could print all of Psalm 104 here, but instead, we can do ourselves a favor by getting out our Bibles, dust-covered or not, and praying this hymn to God the creator. And while we have it open we'll be glad that Fr. F., with all the enthusiasm he is capable of, urges that we read chapters 26, 38, 39, 40, and 41 of the Book of Job.

"Where were you," God asks Job (and us), "when I laid the foundation of the earth?" (38:4) God then lists in magnificent poetry many elements of his creation. "Where were you," God asks, "when I created?" Each day when we open our eyes and see creation, there we can hear God asking the same question. Our response must be the same as Job's: humility. And then our morning prayer will be the prayer of the three young men in the fiery furnace as they call upon all of creation to praise the Lord (Dn 3:52-90).

Even the famed astronomer Carl Sagan, though he was "personally skeptical about many aspects of revealed religion," called upon science and religion to join hands in preserving the global environment. "Efforts to safeguard and cherish the environment need to be infused with a vision of the sacred," he said. Fr. Bruce Vawter, expert in the Book of Genesis, says that "if Genesis is attended to carefully, we see that it gives every encouragement to the present-day ecologist who believes that the earth has been delivered into man's hands as a sacred trust."

Former President Bush had a plan to plant a billion trees to absorb five percent of the air pollution, but in the third world they'd all be cut down. The Philippines tropical rain forest, a missionary in the Philippines reports, has dwindled from 17.5 million hectares in 1946 to less than 1 million today. The cause? The population of the country has jumped from 7 million at the beginning of this century to over 60 million today. It is expected to double in thirty years. "How will it be possible to feed, clothe, shelter, educate and care for 120 million," he asks, "when, even now, the Philippines has one of the highest rates of malnutrition in Asia and many of the ecosystems have been irreversibly destroyed?" God measured and put limits to the earth. It is not indefinite. Rampant breeding of human beings will destroy it. Birth control is necessary.

I will close this with Fr. Gerard Manley Hopkins' "God's Grandeur" and its breath of hope:

> The world is charged with the grandeur of God.
> It will flame out, like shining from shook foil;
> It gathers to a greatness, like the ooze of oil
> Crushed. Why do men then now not reck his
>   rod?
> Generations have trod, have trod, have trod:
> And all is seared with trade; bleared, smeared
>   with toil;
> And wears man's smudge and shares man's
>   smell: the soil
> Is bare now, nor can foot feel, being shod.
>
> And for all this, nature is never spent;
> There lives the dearest freshness deep down
>   things;
> And though the last lights off the black West
>   went
> Oh, morning, at the brown brink eastward,
>   springs—
> Because the Holy Ghost over the bent
> Worlds broods with warm breast and with ah!
>   bright wings.

Reflection Questions

- Fr. Fehren suggests that graffiti and litter are symptoms of spiritual disease. Do you agree? If so, how would you begin to treat this disease?

- What is the difference between worshipping an object and reverencing it as a creation of God?

- Can you name some objects that you have genuine reverence for? What is it about these objects that move you?

- Fr. Fehren suggests that using birth control is a way of showing reverence for creation. Do you agree? Why or why not?

SEVEN

Time to Retire?

Penitent (Yours Truly): Bless me, Father, for I have sinned.

Confessor: Aha! (*Hopefully*) Against the Sixth Commandment, I suppose.

Yours Truly: Not this time, Father. The Seventh Commandment.

Confessor: (*Bored*) Well, get on with it. What was your sin?

Yours Truly: I stole, Father.

Confessor: (*Impatiently*) What did you steal?

Yours Truly: I stole a magazine from a doctor's office.

Confessor: Those magazines are so old that to steal them is not even a venial sin. That's only an imperfection. Or even an act of charity for the other waiting patients. Unless an antique dealer wanted them. Now gimme a real sin so that you have matter for confession.

Yours Truly: Well, I sent my April column in late to the editor of *U.S. Catholic*.

Confessor: (*Shouting. The people in line outside the confessional listen attentively.*) Now *that's* a mortal sin, a real one! For your penance pray the rosary.

Yours Truly: (*Weakly*) The *whole* rosary?

Confessor: Yes, all fifteen decades. Wait, how many times did you turn your column in late since your last confession?

Yours Truly: (*Meekly*) Three times, Father.

Confessor: That'll be three rosaries for your penance, you rotten recidivist. *Dóminus Noster Jesus Christus te absólvat: et ego auctoritáte ipsius te absólvo—*

Yours Truly: But, that's Latin, Father. English is "in" now. Is a Latin absolution valid?

Confessor: Look, I spent eight years in the seminary studying Latin. I'm not going to waste all that. If the pope of Rome doesn't like it that's his problem. Anyhow, what's good enough for Jesus is good enough for me. And if you interrupt me one more time I'll add another rosary to your penance and invalidate the absolution.

Yours Truly, realizing he'll have to find a religious goods store and buy a rosary, shuts up.

Confessor: *...remissionem peccatorum, augmentum gratiae, et praemium vitae aetérnae. Amen.*

Square foot wooden slide between Confessor and Penitent: *Slam!*

Too late, said penitent realizes that he has been cheated out of the first two of the four prayers in the absolution formula and that he hasn't had a chance to explain the "mitigating circumstances" that may reduce the guilt of a sin. In this case he had been thinking about writing on the notion of "retirement" and the magazine had an article on the "geezer generation." Meaning old geezers (anyone past sixty-five). Like me. And maybe you.

I thought that there might be something in the article that would justify purloining the battered periodical, something that could benefit our readers. But, alas, the article was just a gloomy prognostication that there would be more and more of us old folks around.

It was a doom article, predicting how many people there would be beyond sixty-five in ten years, twenty years, thirty years, etc. So it was not of much help, though I didn't realize it until I got home and could read the article. Maybe I could mitigate my penance by sending the magazine back to the doctor. C.O.D, of course. He can apply to Medicare for reimbursement. I have enough personal horror stories about Medicare Blue Cross Shield to finish this chapter.

I could tell the doctor that I needed the magazine for swatting flies in his waiting room and then forgot to leave it there. But that would be a lie, a sin against the Eighth Commandment (though I could have used the magazine to smash a stray cockroach if I had been fast enough) and then the confessor might have me say another rosary for a penance, but this time in Latin, thought to be the language of Jesus before the vernacular came along. *Ave Maria, gratia plena....*

I wish that there were no age sixty-five, that we could just jump from sixty-four to sixty-six. Then maybe we wouldn't know if we were still Junior Citizens or had become Senior Citizens. What if I don't want to be a Senior Citizen? How come Junior Citizens are not termed "Junior Citizens"? Maybe because it seems silly to still be called "Junior" at age sixty-four. Anyhow, in age I am always senior to those younger than I and am junior to those older than I (of whom I know very few).

I could have killed a few friends, but I didn't because that would have been a sin against the Fifth Commandment and my confessor might have given me a penance recommended by St. Leonard of Port Maurice, the Via Crucis (as he called it) or the Stations of the Cross (as we called it until the devotion nearly died out a few years ago). I don't mind doing the Stations, for I could whip through them in fifteen minutes, but the problem might be finding a new-liturgy remodeled church with the fourteen Stations of the Cross. And we were supposed to do our penance before receiving Holy Commu-

nion. One updated church has the Stations in a mon-
tage on the back wall, but I forget where that church
is. Maybe I could find a church where a Vatican I pastor
has them installed on the circular stairway up to the
balcony. St. Leonard says that the Sovereign Pontiffs
have attached ample indulgences to the Stations, but
if I got too self-indulgent I might lose my puny, ever-
threatened reputation for sanctity, in whose odor I still
hope to die.

The reason, before I get too far astray, for wanting to
kill those friends is that they put on a birthday party
for my sixty-fifth birthday. They had to announce to the
whole world that I was sixty-five! Is that a rite of
passage? It's not in the Holy Bible. They wanted it to
be a surprise party, but I had to buy the booze, so they
had to let me know about it. My protests were to no
avail, for no one listens to us old folks. But I still didn't
kill them because if my penance had been the Stations
of the Cross and even if I found a church with them, I
never trusted the prayer at each station (in my childhood), which ended with the words to God, "and then
do with me what Thou wilt." I never knew what God
might have in mind.

I must admit that I have often practiced doddering
so that I would know how to act in old age. Even without
practice, I knock kitchen cabinet doors against my
head when I open them, and when I reach for a glass I
knock it over. If there is anything to bump into, my
notoriously uncoordinated body heads for it. And you
could say that my mind is already doddering, for this
is the longest introduction to what I am getting around
to saying. It's true. It's taking me a long time to say
what I want to say because I have very little to say about
what I want to say.

And more than that, I fear that I will be misunder-
stood. What's bothering me is the notion of "retirement." I hear it all over the place these days. I don't
know when the term first came into popular usage

(Jesus does not mention it), but the term seems to contain the notion that I've worked hard all my life, I've put in my time, I've raised my kids (who are now married off or financially independent), and now at the age of sixty or sixty-two or sixty-five, I deserve a life of irresponsibility, leisure, pleasure, and self-indulgence.

These are not words used by the retirees of whom I am speaking, but it is the germ of their thought. And it is very sad, for it seems that as they get closer to the inevitable judgment of God, they reflect a weakness in faith and then try to grab everything they can before the certain, oncoming death.

It is also a bad example for young people. Is "retirement" the aim and purpose of life? Make enough money so that I can quit working? Revising the familiar axiom, someone said that work is the curse of the drinking class. We've heard of the greed of the eighties (the 1980s); I hope that there'll be no justification in speaking of the greed of the sixty-fives (those aged sixty and older). I know of one person who retired at sixty-two with an ample pension, and she has five mink coats, three sets of fine china, three sets of silverware, two cars (including a Cadillac, and she can't drive), etcetera. She gives nothing away. And I know of other people who after retirement give nothing to charity, do no help in charitable organizations, and do no volunteer work.

For some it seems as though they had retired also from the spiritual life. I hesitate to speak of this because I know that, for many, retirement has meant the opportunity to take part in daily Mass since they were no longer obligated to get to their jobs. Others feel great because they now have time for charitable works they did not have time for before.

Clara Hale, now eighty-three, still takes in babies born to mothers with AIDS. Father Peter, a Salesian priest, eighty, works with lepers in a Thailand jungle. There is an organization called Grandparents Raising Grandchildren. I know that many retired are living in poverty and there are endless heartening accounts of good works being done by the aging; thus I hope that the trend of seeing work as a curse and only a means of obtaining a self-absorbed life of ease does not grow.

Many people are forced to retire from their job or profession at sixty-five, but retirement can mean a change of work, a change of occupation or lifestyle and a continuing opportunity to do good. Yes, we can get tired of a job or a profession and be glad to retire from it. But even if our work or occupation is tiring, boring or burdensome we must remember, if the work is in itself good and contributes to the good of society, that the work is holy and a means of sanctification.

Getting recycled can be good for the spirit. But good work is always good. Even in the garden of Eden, God settled Adam and told him "to till it and keep it" (Gn 2:15).

St. Paul says,

> You know for yourselves that I worked with my own hands to support myself and my companions. In all this I have given you an example that by such work we must support the weak, remembering the words of the Lord Jesus, for he himself said, "It is more blessed to give than to receive" (Acts 20:34-35).

He urges honest labor so that we have something to give to those in need (Eph 4:28).

Many years ago there was an advertisement for car tires that pictured a young boy in a sleeping gown. He was holding a candle and was obviously tired. The ad, using a pun, asked, "Time to re-tire?" The answer for us is "No" if we believe Jesus when he solemnly assures us who hear his word and have faith in the One who sent him that we possess eternal life (Jn 5:24).

Reflection Questions

- When people ask your age, do you: 1) lie about it 2) make a joke and don't tell them 3) tell them but wish they hadn't asked 4) pretend you don't hear them 5) tell them straightforwardly. What are your feelings about getting older?

- What did Fr. Fehren mean by "retirement is a bad example for young people." Do you agree?

- Name those whose "retirement" you admire. What is it that you admire about their behavior?

- Are you attracted or resistant to retirement? What is it about retirement that attracts or repulses you?

EIGHT

The Supreme Law[*]

"They read the gospels and found them difficult, so they turned to religion."

I read that once and for the life of me I cannot recall who said it. It may sound cynical but that does not mean that there is no truth in the statement. To belong to a religion is easier than being religious, easier than following Christ. Jesus promised that his yoke would be easy and his burden light, but most of us don't find his way very easy.

In truth, most of us are born into a religion; our parents bring us up in their religion, church or belief. If we were Catholic we were raised in an obsessively authoritarian institution. Everything in matters religious was decided for us. Some people like that, for it gives them a sense of security. And they can remain children. No need to grow and mature and make decisions. No need to explore the ways of following Jesus.

No need to love.

No need to love God with heart, soul and mind. No need to love your neighbor as yourself. It is easier to follow rules than it is to follow Jesus.

---

[*] Cicero: "Salus populi suprema est lex" ("The welfare of the people is the supreme law"). *The Code of Canon Law*, canon 1752: "...the salvation of souls, which in the Church must always be the supreme law."

Since the church is a society no one is opposed to some rules, but the rules tend to take over. When church laws were first collected into one book in 1917, there were 2,414! Jesus had condemned the Pharisees for making so many laws ("They tie up heavy burdens, hard to bear, and lay them on the shoulders of others" [Mt 23:4]), but *The Code of Canon Law* out-Phariseed the Pharisees.

In 1983 a revision cut the number of laws to 1,752. Imagine the popularity of Jesus if he had been out preaching those to the multitude. Instead he said, "Woe to you, scribes and Pharisees, hypocrites! For you tithe mint, dill, and cummun, and have neglected the weightier matters of the law: justice and mercy and faith" (Mt 23:23).

The 1917 code lists 39 cases in which automatic excommunication is incurred (6 in the new code), but only God can excommunicate one from his presence. It would be well if we all knew more church history—in matters of dogmas, laws and biblical interpretations who said what, when, under what conditions, in which culture, and—above all—by what authority? Jesus is the only head of the church. "[God] has put all things under [Christ's] feet and has made him the head over all things for the church" (Eph 1:22).

Yet there are still many Catholics who prefer to shift responsibility, who wall themselves off from Christ and his hard sayings by putting faith in an intermediary, who are more comfortable playing church. One American cardinal said that his chief work as a cardinal was to promote devotion to "the Holy Father." What about Jesus? An archbishop recently in his diocesan paper commended the appointment of another archbishop because "above all, he is completely faithful to our Holy Father." Above devotion to Jesus? The fact that the new archbishop is in "the primatial see in the United States" has an "importance that can hardly be over-emphasized." You have already overemphasized it; any devotion of U.S. Catholics to Jesus is unaffected by the "primatial see."

I mention "his" diocesan paper in the above paragraph, for a diocesan paper is the house organ of the bishop. An editor would not dare suggest a criticism of the teaching or policy of the bishop. How healthful for the church if diocesan papers could be forums for the views and experiences of the laity—and priests and religious, for that matter. They make up the church, but it will never be.

It is as though we could not be trusted with the truth. We need not fear the truth, for Jesus is "the way, and the truth, and the life," and "the truth will make you free" (Jn 14:6; 8:32). "If we live by the Spirit," writes St. Paul, "let us also be guided by the Spirit" (Gal 5:25). There are not two churches, a teaching church and a learning church. All of us in the church learn and teach. Priscilla and Aquila, who were not only lay people but women, explained in St. Paul's day to Apollos of Ephesus, an authority on Scripture, "the Way of the Lord" (Acts 18:25).

I may again be accused of "a tirade against the pope." My answer: tirade, no; facts, yes. Pius X said, "The masses [of Catholics] have no right or authority except that of being governed, like an obedient flock that follows its Shepherd." Despite Vatican II, that attitude has returned to Rome today, but U.S. Catholics are not buying it. It has, though, caused a loss of morale among U.S. Catholics. And elsewhere.

We see this uneasiness and frustration expressed in a number of books and articles today. Monsignor S.J. Adamo of the Camden diocese wrote on the occasion of his forty-fifth anniversary as a priest that we are sliding back to a pre-Vatican II church. "Vatican II raised hopes for a Catholic Church that would be more democratic—as the Church was in the first centuries," he wrote. "Pleas for women priests and optional celibacy fell on deaf ears. Not for any strong moral reason but simply because the Vatican felt the traditions were unreformable. Discipline took precedence over the wishes of the people of God. Better to have no Masses, insisted the hierarchy, than to have married men stand at the altar—as Apostles Peter and James once did."

A new Swiss Catholic paper whose subtitle is *Forum for an Open Church* is growing swiftly in circulation. In it a moral theologian writes, "Solidarity with the church does not mean blind obedience. Where, when and how the teaching against birth control is supposed to have been confirmed by God in revelation remains a total mystery."

I am not a bookseller, but there are some recent books that I recommend to discouraged Catholics, to Catholics who are bitter about insensitive authoritarianism in church officials, to Catholics who are voting with their feet and not taking part in church activity.

Church: Charism and Power (Crossroad) by Father Leonardo Boff. Read it; you'll love it. "Sacred power lies within the entire community, and not only in the hands of a few."

Jesus before Christianity (Orbis) by Father Albert Nolan. "Jesus did not found an organization; he inspired a movement. He remains present and active through the presence and activity of his Spirit (2 Cor 3:17-18)."

A Catholic Bill of Rights (Sheed & Ward) edited by Leonard Swidler and Herbert O'Brien. "All Catholics have the right to a voice in all decisions that affect them, including the choosing of their leaders."

The Churches the Apostles Left Behind (Paulist) by Father Raymond Brown, S.S. "At one time or other every Christian is or should be part of the teaching church and everyone should be part of the learning church. Some lay people are quite capable of being teachers themselves, not just transmitting what they received but making their own contribution."

The Marginal Catholic—Challenge, Don't Crush (Ave Maria Press) by Father Joseph Champlin. "Divorced and remarried couples in great numbers, with and without church approbation, consider themselves good Catholics and do not hesitate to come forward for communion." Fr. Champlin is an experienced pastor of many years. I wonder if we don't have more "marginal" Catholics than parish-enrolled Catholics today.

Many marginal Catholics come to see me. I have not found one who was angry at Jesus; all have been hurt, angered or frustrated by clergy and bishops for whom man-made rules seem to be more important than the compassion of Jesus. "Avoid making Mass attendance a requirement for baptism....We possess no serious research which can determine whether marital preparation programs prevent bad marriages or not....We cannot judge or categorize the inner religious state of another individual."

He repeats the old theological truth, which some lay people seem slow to learn, that "the bride and groom minister the sacrament to each other," and he asks, "Should they not also be the persons to judge their readiness to receive this gift?" Champlin's book reflects the advice of St. Paul: "Let your gentleness be known to everyone" (Phil 4:5).

Finally, *Why You Can Disagree and Remain a Faithful Catholic* (Meyer-Stone) by Father Philip Kaufman, O.S.B. "How valuable is a teaching authority that for over 1,400 years not only failed to instruct Catholics on the gross immorality of slavery, but by official teaching actively supported it?" This is a carefully researched book, direct and to the point on, among other things, birth control, divorce and remarriage, democracy in the church and "infallible teaching."

"Is it moral to deny the possibility of remarriage to those whose first marriages have irreparably ended? The right to the Eucharist is a fundamental right of the baptized, not a privilege granted by the hierarchy, but a gift offered to his own by the Lord of the church."

These books are signs of healthy ferment in the church and certainly are a help and comfort to confused, disaffected, disillusioned and alienated Catholics.

It is heartening to see that American bishops did wide consultation before issuing a couple of their documents—although one *New York Times* headline once read, "Bishops Take Harder Line in a Statement on Women's Issues." The bishop of Milwaukee, however, had a number of sessions with women in which he listened to their views on abortion. *U.S. Catholic* magazine consults its readers every month.

From books, magazines and newspapers I have dozens and dozens of clippings which give evidence that Catholics do not want to be treated as dummies in matters of faith. Some call for *perestroika* in the church, some call for Catholicism with a human face, some yearn for the earliest days of the church when "the apostles and the elders, *with the consent of the whole church*" made decisions (Acts of the Apostles 15:22; emphasis added).

In one issue of the *New York Times*, 4,500 Catholics signed an ad calling for reform in the church. Maybe they were inspired by St. Bernard of Clairvaux, who reminded Pope Eugene III that "you are not the lord of bishops, but one of their number." Pope Clement VIII had a simple Italian miller tortured and put to death because his opinion in a matter of cosmology was different. At least we don't have to worry about that anymore—though we could lose our job if we work for the church.

St. Paul asks us, "Does God supply you with the Spirit and work miracles among you by your doing the works of the law, or by your believing what you heard?" (Gal 3:5)

Still troubled? Listen to Jesus. "Very truly, I tell you, anyone who hears my word and believes him who sent me has eternal life" (Jn 5:24).

Now.

Reflection Questions

- Fr. Fehren suggests that marginal Catholics are angry at the church, not at Jesus. Does this ring true for you?

- Fr. Fehren speaks of a cardinal whose mission was to spread devotion to the pope. How should the pope fit into our lives?

- Fr. Fehren makes many remarks about the importance of lay people (as opposed to the hierarchy) to the church. Are you comfortable with this position?

- If you had your way, would there be more or fewer regulations in the church?

NINE

Stone Soup

"**I** am hungry," said the young stranger to the older woman who had opened the door in response to his knock. "Could you please give me something to eat."

"I'm sorry," said the woman. "I have nothing to give you."

"Well, then," said the young traveler, "could you at least give me a stone?"

"A stone?" said the woman. "There are plenty here. Take one from the ground. What will you do with that?"

"I will make stone soup," said the young man.

"Soup?" said the woman. "How will you do that?"

"First I need some boiling water and then I will make soup from the stone."

Intrigued, the woman allowed the man into her house and she furnished him with a pot of water which was then set to boil. "It would taste a little better," said the young man, if there were a carrot in there." So the woman put a carrot in the pot.

"An onion would add a lot to the flavor," said the young man. And the woman dropped an onion into the pot.

"It smells delicious," said the woman approvingly.

"Come to think of it, though," said the young man, "it would smell even better if we had a rutabaga in it."

So the woman found a rutabaga in her larder and added it to the concoction.

And thus it went, with the woman, who supposedly had nothing to give, adding more and more things to the soup. When the soup was done, they both sat down to eat it. They finished it to and including the last drop—except for the stone. When the young man prepared to leave, he took the stone.

"What will you do with that?"

"It is not boiled enough yet," said the young man, "so I will take it along for my next bowl of soup."

So you've heard this story before? In elementary school? In a children's book of stories? Well, I had never heard it until I was on an Amtrak train going from Baltimore to New York on Easter Tuesday. In former times, Easter Monday was, for clergy, called Emmaus Day. We priests had supposedly worked to exhaustion during Holy Week and Easter and were thus entitled to take Easter Monday off in accordance with the gospel account of the two disciples going to Emmaus on Easter Sunday afternoon (Lk 24:13). We were expected to go visiting, so I went to Baltimore to visit a Lutheran pastor and his French wife. She is a gourmet chef, so this kind of ecumenism was most rewarding. The weather was perfect there, but it rained on the three-hour ride home and I had picked up a cold, which affected my eyes and prevented me from reading.

Thus I heard from the seats behind me a grandmother reading a story to her restless grandson. The book from which she read called the story "The Soup of Stone." I listened intently to every word.

On my return I telephoned a kindergarten teacher. "Everyone knows that story," she said. "You can find it in any bookstore." So I went to several bookstores and it was not there. I then went to the children's section of the bookstore department of Macy's. "It's a classic," said a clerk, "but we don't have it." A children's classic? Ah, my lost childhood. I had been deprived.

Off I went to the mid-Manhattan branch of the New York Public Library. It was not there! Well, so what. What interested me is that the story sounded like one of Christ's parables. He often told a story and then let the listeners think about it. And I thought about the soup of stone. What was the point of it? One version tells of three young men who went from village to village and got free food by this ruse.

My first thought on hearing the story was somewhat pious. It is that we may think we have nothing to give but we all have something to give. Jesus in his poverty seemed to have nothing to give. What a nothing he appeared to be. Born in a stable, of poor parents in a little town in a conquered nation. No political, financial or social power. He had only one thing to give—himself—and he gave it. The old woman in the story said that she had nothing to give, yet she gave one thing after another to the nourishing soup.

If we say we that we have nothing to give, we are lying. We have ourselves to give. An onion, a rutabaga, some meat, some spices—we are a variety of things that can become our gifts for the nourishment of others. And our love is the thing that no one else can give for us.

Pietistic, yes, but realistic.

I also thought of Christ's words, "Is there anyone among you who, if your child asks for bread, will give a stone?" (Mt 7:9) Sometimes, though, when we ask God for bread he seems to give us a stone. I know from experience that God sometimes seemed to give me a stone and then I found out later that he really was giving me bread. I suspect that we have all had that experience. We know that God loves us, so we must trust his wisdom.

The old woman in the story gave a stone but it became nourishing soup.

My next reaction was to recall that recently I had sat in a full theater one half block off Broadway, listening not just to a story or a parable but to the whole gospel of St. Mark. The audience was not a Christian or a religious group; it was made up of regular theater-goers. They had paid for their tickets and they sat there fascinated as Alec McCowan, a British actor, simply read the gospel. They did not even leave at the inter-mission.

McCowan was on the stage alone. He did the reading but Jesus was the star. I think that it had a run of two months. There were no deletions or additions or com-ments or explanations. He just read the gospel as is. McCowan picked St. Mark's gospel, he said, because he found it the most narrative.

I hope that parents in these days of TV still read to their children, as the grandmother did on the train. But I wonder how often Catholic parents read Bible stories to their children. Or even read directly from the Bible to them. I read the gospels at Sunday Mass for more than forty-two years, but for the first time I had a lesson in how to read the gospels. Compared to McCowan, reading with great intelligence, my reading is a mono-tone—through my nose. The only thing that kept the congregation awake is that they were standing.

There is an account of a preacher who after reading the gospel to the yawns of the congregation announced a story about a donkey. Everyone's ears perked up, and the preacher told the congregation that they were more interested in a donkey than they were in Jesus. But perhaps his reading of the gospel was as monotonous as the braying of a donkey. If his voice indicated a lack of interest, then how could his congregation be inter-ested? I learned something from McCowan.

Anyhow, to make a long parable short, I decided to read one of the gospels straight through, from begin-ning to end, at one sitting. No stopping for meditation or exegesis. I chose John's gospel, considered more lofty or theological than the others. And it was a fasci-nating read!

Try it sometime. It is not the usual way to read the gospels. It is better, of course, to read a short passage and reflect on it. Reading passages in a small group, reflecting on the passage and discussing it, has become the salvation of the church in Latin American countries. "What is Jesus saying to us here, now, in our situation?" they ask.

After reading John's gospel I wondered why Jesus was so alive in those pages. First we must credit the gospel writers. They were good writers; any novelist could learn something from them.

Then I realized that Jesus was out on the streets with people, in the synagogue, in the temple, and in homes with them. He listened to them and responded to them. He ate with them, sweated with them, got his feet dusty with them. He went to them, and because he went to them, they came to him and listened to him. He was not ensconced in a palace. He was not protected by Plexiglas. He did not fly first class. He did not give himself pompous titles. He touched them, placed his hands on them, lifted them up, washed their feet.

Even in the gospel of John, Jesus is directly engaged with people. He is there where they are. He asks questions. In John's gospel I counted about thirty-three questions. I wrote down each question. It is a good spiritual experience just to answer those questions, perhaps one each day. Just sense the presence of Jesus and listen to him, through the gospel, ask us the question. We must answer. No, don't run away, don't avoid or evade, don't turn to something else.

"What are you looking for?" That is the first question that Jesus asks in John's gospel (1:38). That's a big question, a deeply philosophical and religious question. It may take a long time to answer. What am I looking for in my life?

"Woman, what concern is that to you?" (2:4) Jesus asks this question of Mary when, like a good Jewish mother, she is concerned about the shortage of wine at a wedding feast. When we see poverty, homelessness, suffering, Jesus asks us, "How does this concern you?" A peasant woman in El Salvador says, "For every gun you send here a child dies." "How does that concern you?" Jesus asks us. My tax money buys those guns and sends them to the military in El Salvador. What concern is that of mine? Let Cain answer: "Am I my brother's keeper?" (Gn 4:9)

Why did I ever read this gospel?

To Jesus' questions there are no facile answers. We must reflect before we answer. Even to such questions as "Do you want to be made well?" (5:6) Yes, my faith is often shaken. Feel abandoned? Jesus asks, "Did I not choose you?" (6:70) Think there is no hope, everything is finished, gone, nothing to live for? "Why are you weeping?" (20:15) Jesus asks this on the day of his resurrection. On Friday he had been crucified. For his followers this seemed the end of everything, total disaster, all hope and expectancy smashed, no future. When we are at the end of our rope, Jesus asks, "Why are you weeping?"

His most important, personal and touching question: "Do you love me?" (21:15)

Questions, questions, questions. All four gospels come alive with the questions of Jesus.

What good is a stone?

It may become nourishing soup. Or a cornerstone (Mt 21:42).

Reflection Questions

- Have you ever thought that you had no gift to give anyone? Fr. Fehren suggests that you did have a gift to give even in those moments. What was it?

- Have you ever thought that when you asked for bread God gave you a stone? When? Did you find out later that God really gave you bread?

- Look at some of the questions posed in John's gospel (pages 60-61). Which ones are easy to answer? Which ones are difficult? Spend some time with the difficult ones.

TEN

Lord of Mercy and Compassion

Once upon a time I wrote an article for a Catholic magazine in which I included the following paragraph, pertinent to what I was writing about:

> If our life is a gift from God it is something that we own, the only thing that we really own. Why cannot we then terminate it if we wish? It seems that some of the early martyrs practically committed suicide, a death they could in faith have avoided, had they not so zealously wished to be with Jesus in heaven. Jesus could have avoided his own death (Mt 26:53). Was his death a "mercy killing?" He allowed himself to be killed because he had mercy on us.

The editor, in deciding to excise the paragraph, was kind and thoughtful enough to telephone me and tell my why he was cutting out the paragraph. He thought that the readers were not yet ready for the ideas expressed in the paragraph. The buck stops at the editor's desk, and I have no complaints about his decision. I agree that perhaps too much was put too succinctly into one paragraph. For the reader there was not sufficient preparation in the preceding text for comments that were, to some, unconventional.

To look at the first point: "Life is evidently the gift of God" says the Rahner-Vorgrimmler *Theological Dictionary*. If it is a gift, it is a gift. If I give a gift to someone and the person accepts it, the gift it no longer mine and I have no more ownership or control of it. There are no strings attached to any real gift. Thus, if God gives me life as a gift it is my life; I possess it. I may mis-use that gift, as we all do, but I must have the freedom to do so or I am reduced to being an animal and am no longer in the image and likeness of God.

Though the life may be "solitary, poor, nasty, brutish and short" (Hobbes), it is mine. Job, on losing his family and possessions, said, "The Lord gave and the Lord has taken away; blessed be the name of the Lord!" But is God held to a lesser standard in the matter of gift-giving? I don't have answers; I am only wondering about these things. At least the revised code of canon law has erased the former penalty of denying Christian burial to suicides.

The matter of ending one's own life is more pressing today, for, unlike the past when people just died naturally, we now have and use complicated and expensive means of dragging out the lives of even those who are fatally ill. If I am suffering, in great pain and agony, in an illness that I know is hopeless, no chance of recovery, knowing that this hopeless medical "care" is costing thousands upon thousands of dollars, may I not decide to end this bodily life?

It has been taught that "extraordinary means" need not be used to extend a life, but have the "extraordinary means" of the past become the "ordinary means" of today? If it is my life, cannot I make decisions about it? Have I any rights over my own body? I know that my spirit or soul will live on; I will live on. Must I suffer for the sake of suffering? And if I anticipate this condition, may I not appoint someone to make the decision for me if I become mentally incompetent?

God cannot be a sadist; God must the be the "Lord of mercy and compassion," according to an old Catholic hymn. A dear friend of mine, in his seventies, ended his earthly life this past year. He had cancer of the bone marrow, there was no cure, he was suffering from agonizing treatments, and he knew that he was incurable. From his years of treatment, he had saved enough pills to end his bodily functions. He consulted his children, all adult, and his wife. They agreed. He took the pills and died quietly and with dignity.

His family remembered this passage from the book of Wisdom:

> But the souls of the righteous are in the hand of
>   God,
> and no torment will ever touch them.
> In the eyes of the foolish they seemed to have
>   died,
> and their departure was thought to be a disaster,
> and their going from us to be their destruction;
> but they are at peace (3:1-3).

Dick, my friend, was aware of what Patrick Keegan, the saintly leader of Catholic Action in England, said on his deathbed a few days before he died: "I am madly in love with my Beloved, and raring to go." And that is reminiscent of St. Paul, who said,

> For to me, living is Christ and dying is gain. If I
> am to live in the flesh, that means fruitful labor
> for me; and I do not know which I prefer. I am
> hard pressed between the two: my desire is to
> depart and be with Christ, for that is far better
> (Phil 1:21-23).

Because he was healthy and productive, he knew that it was more urgent to continue his apostolic work.

He wasn't brain-dead and didn't have ten tubes and wires attached to a machine keeping him "alive."

"The wind is old and still at play / While I must hurry upon my way / For I am running to Paradise," wrote the Irish poet William Butler Yeats. He was echoing St. Cyprian, who said,

> Run forward to see at once our fatherland and to greet our parents. A huge number of those dear friends are waiting there for us. What great delight will be ours and theirs when we come into their sight and embrace! What nameless joy in that heavenly kingdom, where there is no dread of dying, but only everlasting life! To these folk, my dear friends, we must hurry on with ardent desire. We must hope to be living with them soon, so that we may the sooner come to Christ.

And that is the second point of the obliterated paragraph. Some historians and hagiographers wonder whether all that martyrdom of the early centuries was necessary. Did a routine civic duty necessarily mean a denial of faith and thus provide an avenue to having one's life ended so one could be fully united with Christ in his kingdom? Were some martyrs, in effect, suicides for the sake of being fully with Christ in heaven?

Jesus could have prevented his death, the third point in the paragraph. When the mob armed with swords and clubs came to Gethsemane, Peter, in an effort to protect Jesus, slashed at the servant of the high priest and cut off his ear. Jesus told Peter to put his sword back and then said, "Do you think that I cannot appeal to my Father, and he will at once send me more than twelve legions of angels?" (Mt 26:53). Out of mercy for us, Jesus allowed himself to be killed.

The word "euthanasia" suggests for some people a diabolic evil, a license to slaughter malformed children, the mentally retarded and the aged. I have read that the "birth control mentality" (whatever that is) leads to approval of birth control, abortion and mercy killing. That's stupid. The word "euthanasia" comes from the Greek for "good death" (*eu* + *thanatos*).

One Catholic newspaper, in an article condemning merciful death, once quoted the Florida bishops: "We can never justify the withdrawal of sustenance on the basis of the quality of life of the patient." Does the patient in useless, endless pain and agony have anything to say about it? Are we respecting his life? I watched a dear friend, mind gone, too weak to move, no hope of recovery, tortured to death by his doctor. I finally got a durable power of attorney to stop it. Yes, the nutrition tubes were still in, but he died quietly. I wonder if some of the anti-euthanasia people believe in mercy or in an afterlife, or that Jesus has prepared a place for us (Jn 14:2).

In 1990, sixteen of the eighteen Texas bishops said that

> the morally appropriate forgoing or withdrawing
> of artificial nutrition and hydration from a
> permanently unconscious person is not
> abandoning that person. Rather, it is accepting
> the fact that the person has come to the end of
> his or her pilgrimage and should not be impeded
> from taking the final step.

Only Satan, wanting to keep people from eternal bliss, would prevent that.

Even Pius XII long ago said, "It is unnatural to prevent death in instances where there is no hope of recovery. When nature is calling for death there is no question that one can remove the life support systems."

How about "Thou shalt not kill," the Fifth "Commandment"? There is no reference to the "Ten Commandments" in Scripture. They were called the "words" of God, describing not absolute moral laws but a way for the Hebrew community to live with God. They were not given for the world at large. Thus the fifth "word" forbade only the murder of another Jew. The Hebrew word used here for "kill" has no exact English translation. Women could be stoned to death for adultery, and the Hebrews killed thousands of men, women and children in their conquest of the "promised" land.

Later these ten subjects become the basis of moral law for both Jews and Christians, though Jesus, quoting the Jewish Bible, said that love of God and neighbor should be the guide for our way of life. St. Thomas says that this "commandment" forbids detraction and anger (anger impedes reason, justice and mercy). The Catechism of the Council of Trent says that love of neighbor, patience, beneficence, mildness and forgiveness of injuries is mandated, hatred and revenge forbidden.

"Respect Life" says a cheap, ugly banner over the main entrance of an expensive, lavish Park Avenue Catholic church. That sounds nice. I piously pass on. But then I wonder: What life, what forms of life, whose life? Then I remember a TV news scene in which a reporter following the pope's recent trip to Mexico asks a woman living in a tin shack with her nine undernourished, sickly children why she has so many children. She answers, "Because the pope said that birth control is a mortal sin." Respect life?

There are a thousand ways of being anti-human life. We all have our own ways. Perhaps paying taxes so that our President can send the money to the El Salvador military for killing thousands of innocent people. Perhaps driving a car when not absolutely necessary—the car in one year will release its own weight in carbon into the atmosphere.

A bishop on the National Conference of Catholic Bishops' Committee for Pro-Life Activities is worried about a "new anti-child campaign directed at low-income and minority families." I invite that bishop to be pro-life and feed and educate those nine Mexican chil-

children. Or any of the 1,500 children who die *every hour* from hunger-related causes.

"Pro-life" is the simplistic slogan of the anti-abortionists. I don't know of anyone who is simplistically pro-abortion. I am glad to hear that some "pro-lifers" are doing something to help children after birth. Archbishop Weakland of Milwaukee, after listening to women throughout their archdiocese, commented on the "narrowness of vision on the part of some of the pro-life people."

"Conception is a process," he says, "not a moment."

When I was a pastor in a rural parish, a husband telephoned to say that his wife had experienced an involuntary abortion. Would I come over and baptize the fetus. For their consolation, I rushed over, held the fetus (which looked like a little sausage) in my hand, turned on the kitchen faucet and gave it conditional (as we called it then) baptism.

I agree with Archbishop Weakland that arranged abortion is a very complicated ethical, medical, moral and emotional problem. As he says, there are no glib answers. A suggestion: Read John Steinbeck's novel *Of Mice and Men*. Lennie, an innocent, retarded ranch hand is about to be lynched. His worker buddy can unobtrusively end his life before the terror, suffering and pain of the lynching. Would you do it after you've sung the hymn, "Lord of Mercy and Compassion"?

Reflection Questions

- Would you ever consider ending your own life? Under what circumstances?

- When you read about the terminally ill man who took his own life (page 65), did you feel supportive, angry, or fearful?

- What would you like from the church on this issue?

- What do you think about martyrs? Is there a difference between the martyrs described on page 66 and modern martyrs such as Archbishop Oscar Romero? Does knowing about people who have died for their faith affect your own faith? If so, how?

- Have you made out a living will? What went into your decision?

- If we have the opportunity to save ourselves, shouldn't we do so? If Jesus could have saved himself, shouldn't he have done so?

- Do you have different viewpoints about allowing a person to die versus a person directly taking his or her own life? If so, how do your views differ?

ELEVEN

I Thee Wed

I get requests. "Father, would you please write about marriage."

"You write about it," I feel like answering. "You're married, I'm not."

Or a couple will come in and say, "Father, we'd like to get married. Whatta we hafta do?"

"Whatta ya wanna do?" I answer. "It's your wedding, not mine."

"Well, what are the requirements? Don't we have to get permissions, dispensations, delegations, authorizations, and furnish certificates of baptism, first communion, and confirmation, and fill out forms and promise not to practice birth control and ask the parish music director what music we may have at the ceremony and wait a year even if we have been living together for five years and, at great expense (rent being what it is), separate for a year and even if we are a widow and a widower sixty years old aren't we forced to take the Pre-Cana conferences so that we can have a priest at our wedding? Didn't Jesus say so?"

No, my dear trusting, down-trodden, brow-beaten, devout, badly-educated-in-the-faith Catholics, Jesus did not say so. Canon lawyers may get their rocks off on these petty legalisms or indulge in them as one does in a banana split or a hot fudge sundae, but don't confuse them with Jesus, who condemned some Pharisees for empowering themselves with paper prescriptions to make the faithful cower in fear for their eternal salvation.

Certificates? Why don't we trust you? In these days when Catholics are leaving the institution by the hundreds of thousands we priests should be happy that you come to us and ask us to assist in your wedding. I know one Catholic woman who was married to the same man for sixty-five years, until death did them part, and she never received the sacrament of confirmation. Marriage is a sacrament which lay people give to each other; they are the ministers of the sacrament. They, not the priest, make the vows.

Marriage is where the lay people should be the boss. They have the authority, the authenticity, the expertise, the experience. Yes, they often fail, as we see by the divorce rate, but we priests do too. We priests don't own any of the sacraments and we especially don't own marriage. We should be willing to help in any way we can, but we should be leery about laying down stringent conditions undreamed of by Christ.

"Feed my lambs," said Jesus — don't hurt them.

"Feed my sheep," said Jesus — don't throw them out.

Inflexible mandatory conditions can turn what should be a joyful time into one of frustration and bitterness. As Father Joseph Champlin says, these forced pre-marital procedures "run perilously close to violating the couples' natural right to marry." He adds that "we possess no serious research which can determine whether marital preparation programs prevent bad marriages or not."

Promises? What good are forced promises? In the matter of children, only the married couple can determine what is best for their own family. Everyone else is an outsider. In good conscience the couple will do what is best for their family and God will be with them. One couple went to their pastor to arrange for marriage. The man had a terrible speech defect worse than stuttering. His doctors told him that any children born of him would have the same affliction. They love children and expected to adopt some, but knew the cruelty of having some of their own. Unless you promise to have children, the priest thundered at them, I will not preside at your wedding and you cannot have it here. With a heavy heart they left, wondering about Jesus' invitation, "Come to me, all you that are weary and are carrying heavy burdens, and I will give you rest" (Mt 11:28).

Fr. Karl Rahner's *Encyclopedia of Theology*, after pointing out that "God joins the marriage partners together," says that the church "must not interfere with the freedom to marry, or obscure the fact that bride and groom themselves contract the marriage, by any undue perfectionism."

"But the marriage must take place in a 'sacred place'—a church or a temple—doesn't it?" Some bishops have intruded on the freedom of couples in their own sacrament to decree that the ceremony must take place in a "sacred place." But if God created the world, the world is sacred, a fact being recognized these days in our new emphasis on ecology.

Many couples today like to be married in a garden, as Adam and Eve were. Gardens are often more beautiful today than the "sacred" church stripped of its charm, warmth and history and turned into a barn for the "new" liturgy. If the pope can have Mass in a baseball field, why can't a marriage, considered less excellent than the Eucharist, take place outside a church building? Masses are often held in homes these days.

Many couples like to have the wedding where the reception is going to be because, in this age of mobility, families and friends are scattered all over the country, and if they first must find the place of the ceremony and then later find the reception place, they usually skip the ceremony and just go to the reception. Did the wedding at Cana take place in the synagogue? All we know is that Jesus was at the reception, where he furnished gallons and gallons of wine. Marriage is an event, not a place.

"But will the church recognize my marriage if I don't follow all these recent man-made regulations?" You recognize your own marriage, I hope, because you make the vows and administer the sacrament. I recognize the marriage. Your family and friends recognize the marriage. We know from polls and surveys that most U.S. Catholics recognize the marriage. The state recognizes the marriage. The church is 800 million Catholics around the world. It's impossible to get word to all of them so that they can decide whether to "recognize" your marriage or not.

"If I don't follow in detail the recent man-made regulations, will God be present at my wedding?" That is up to God. No one can keep God from your wedding. "Again, truly I tell you, if two of you agree on earth about anything you ask, it will be done for you by my Father in heaven. For where two or three are gathered in my name, I am there among them" (Mt 18:19-20).

"Will I be excommunicated?" No one can excommunicate you from God. God tends to "incommunicate" people. Anyhow, God can make up his own mind about whether he still loves you or not. Because of a local problem, St. Paul told parishioners not to associate with any Christian who was immoral, covetous, an idolater, an abusive person, a drunkard or a thief, and not even to eat with them (1 Cor 5:11). He was appealing to the people, not to one "authority." If we tried that today, the pews would be far emptier than they are now. And we could forget about forgiving "seven times seventy times."

Again because of a local situation, whoever wrote the second epistle of John—an "elder"—after speaking beautifully of love, recommended to Christians: "Do not receive into the house or welcome anyone who comes to you and does not bring this teaching [of Christ]; for to welcome is to participate in the evil deeds of such a person" (vv 10-11). That would be a kind of excommunication, by the people, not by an official, which would spell the end of any kind of ecumenism in our day.

"But isn't the pope the vicar of Christ?" The bishop of Rome is not *the* vicar of Christ; he is *a* vicar of Christ and so are you. We once had three popes at one time and they all excommunicated each other. People who charged interest were excommunicated, but now the Vatican bank does it.

Among the popes were married men, murderers, sadists, sodomites, heretics, fornicators, simoniacs (buyers and sellers of church offices). One pope was sixteen years old. One turned the Lateran palace (where popes lived before the Vatican) into a whorehouse. Would you take their excommunications seriously? I wonder if God pays any attention.

"But a Holy Father?" Some of the "Holy Fathers" were not so holy, but then neither are some of us. And sometimes they were not fatherly. But many were very saintly, and there may have been a few martyrs among them. Jesus did not go around proclaiming himself holy. He eschewed titles.

I often wish that Catholics knew more church history. From the pulpit and the Catholic press we do not get much of it—perhaps an effort to protect us from loss of faith. But this knowledge would be spiritually beneficial. We need never fear the truth. Faith is not an escape from reality. Knowledge of church history would help put our faith where it should be—in Jesus Christ.

"Will my marriage be a sacrament?" The simplest answer: It will be if you make it such. Again, it would be well to know the history of marriage in the church. Theologians are still discussing what makes marriage a sacrament. Father Theodore Mackin, S.J., near the conclusion of three fat scholarly volumes on marriage in the church, says,

75

> Virtually since the beginning of Christian theorizing about marriage, this (discussion) has gone on in dissociation from the experience of marriage.
>
> The theoreticians, all of them male and virtually all celibate monks or clerics, have designed models of marriage in the abstract.
>
> They have designed them tendentiously, in order to clamp them onto real-life marriages so as to make the latter amenable to regulation.
>
> Rarely was married Christians' experience of marriage consulted. Therefore the designers did not know in fact what a marriage is.
>
> But now the authorities, the theologians and the canonists are turning to the married to find out what marriage is—and therefore what the sacrament is.
>
> Better still, more and more the critical examination of marriage is being done by the Christian married themselves.

That second to last line seems a little optimistic in my experience, but hope springs eternal in the human breast.

In the first centuries of the church, marriage was considered a civil affair; the presence of a priest was not necessary. In the first thousand years there was no unanimity among popes, bishops church councils and theologians on marriage. At times and places, divorce and remarriage were officially sanctioned.

I was rash enough to write on marriage once in *U.S. Catholic* magazine (June 1982), and I recommended love, prayer and a sense of humor—qualities necessary in any human relationship.

Reflection Questions

- What was the most beautiful wedding you ever attended? What made it so? What was the most "sacramental" wedding you ever attended? What made it so? Were the two weddings the same?

- What makes a wedding sacred? If you are married, what made your wedding sacred? If it didn't feel sacred, what might have made it so?

- What makes a wedding "Catholic" in your mind?

- Should priests have more or less to say about how weddings are done these days?

- In the first centuries, marriages were civil affairs. The church didn't get involved. What, if anything, is better about Catholic marriages today?

TWELVE

I Was an Altar Boy

Questions. Questions, questions, questions. Boy, do I get questions.

Oops! Is that sexist because I said "Boy"? O.K. Girl, do I get questions. Writers are going batty these days trying to avoid "sexist" language. At a recent Catholic conference, a speaker inadvertently referred to the Holy Spirit as "he" and a number of women shouted at him, "She, she, she."

Oh, gawd, already in the second paragraph I am distracted from what I really want to write about. Well, not what I really *want* to write about but what I eventually must write about. Which is why I welcome distractions.

Why don't I want to write about it? Because the question is almost too big and too deep to answer. And I don't have all the answers. Even Jesus didn't give all the specific answers. He just gave us answers from which we could deduct specific answers for the specific questions we have for our particular time, experience and place.

Questions that I am asked: Can one have an honest relationship with God? What does it mean to forgive? How does one get to heaven? What does it mean to pray? What is the meaning of grace? What is the meaning of hell? How can I lead my life more fully?

And, lately, the most frequent: Why be a Catholic? Or, as one letter expresses it:

> I entered the church through the RCIA [Rite of
> Christian Initiation of Adults] in 1982,
> convinced I had found a home, a place where I
> could worship and serve for the rest of my life. I
> now wonder if the Christian life could be lived
> more fully somewhere else.

The more simple the question, the more difficult the answer. These questions come from concerned, thoughtful people, and glib, professional answers will not do. Even facile answers such as Jesus gave to the Pharisees—"Give therefore to the emporer the things that are the emperor's, and to God the things that are God's" (Mt 22:21)—may not help. He did not give a list of what belonged to Caesar and what belonged to God.

Yes, he was answering people of bad faith who were trying to ensnare him with a politically sensitive question. And it worked. "When they heard this, [the Pharisees] were amazed; and they left him and went away" (Mt 22:22). After thinking it over, however, they may have come back to ask for a more exact and detailed answer.

Years ago, as we know, in catechism classes we learned answers by rote. Everything was cut and dried, and some older Catholics still find security in that. But for most Catholics, that doesn't work today. They are better educated, are more independent, can think for themselves and no longer want to be treated like infants nursing at the breasts of holy mother the church.

Nor will it help for priests to address Catholics as "my son" or "my child." Only fictional priests do that. Last night in a TV story, a priest called an adult woman "my child." And the night before, a movie priest called someone "my son." In more than forty-five years as a priest, I have never called anyone my son or my child. Only a Renaissance pope could do that and mean it.

Again and again and again people tell me, "I quit the church" or "I don't go to church anymore" or "I haven't been to church for a long time." They consider themselves "outside" the church, yet all consider themselves Catholic.

They will tell me of their Catholic education — in elementary school, high school and college. The sentence I hear most often is, "I was an altar boy." When I hear that, I know what is coming next. Why do they tell me? They still miss something about the church, something more than nostalgia. They expect a response from me or they would not tell me.

Some say, "I'm still Catholic, I'll always be Catholic, but I'm not a practicing Catholic." They will say, "I was born and raised Catholic." If they have children they usually want them baptized Catholic. We used to call them "lapsed" Catholics or "fallen-away" Catholics. Now we use a gentler term, "marginal" Catholics. A few have joined Protestant religions because they felt more wanted there.

Sometimes when they confide in me, it is almost as if they were challenging me to explain to them why they should remain in the church or stay Catholic. And that is the difficult question. First, each person is different and has had a different experience in the church. Second, there usually isn't time to bring them up to date on biblical studies, theology, and church history, and to show them that every word that comes from the Vatican, the chancery office, the pulpit or the rectory is not necessarily from the mouth of Jesus.

Third, though we often use the words "Catholic" and "church" frequently, we do so without exactly defining them. Perhaps we should do what Stephen Dedalus in James Joyce's *A Portrait of the Artist as a Young Man* does: explore the meaning of words we commonly use. When his fellow students in a boarding school ask

Stephen if he kisses his mother before he goes to school, he says yes and they laugh at him. So he says that he doesn't and they laugh again. And he asks himself, "What did that mean, to kiss?"

What is the church? What does it mean to be Catholic? It seems logical that only if we know what the church is can we consider leaving it or remaining in it. Only if we know what it means to be a Catholic can we consider ourselves Catholic or not. Theologian Fr. Avery Dulles, S.J., in his book *Models of the Church* says that Christians "are not agreed about what the Church really is."

He agrees with the constitution on the Church of the Second Vatican Council that the church is a "mystery." In fact, the constitution's first chapter is titled "The Mystery of the Church." A footnote in the Herder and Herder edition of the council documents points out that "the term 'mystery' indicates that the Church, as a divine reality inserted into history, cannot be fully captured by human thought or language."

At the opening of the second session, Paul VI said, "The Church is a mystery. It is a reality imbued with the hidden presence of God. It lies, therefore, within the very nature of the Church to be always open to new and greater exploration."

To get a better understanding of this mystery, Dulles lists five models of the church: the church as institution, as mystical communion, as sacrament, as herald and as servant. The problem is that many Catholics who say that they are fed up with the church and want to leave the church see the church merely as an institution. That juridical or societal model, says Dulles, was dominant from 1600 to 1940. It identifies the church with the hierarchy, who juridicize and institutionalize teaching and in "sanctifying" the flock act like "engineers opening and shutting the valves of grace." In this model, "all power is conceived as descending from the pope."

We cannot find a solid base in Scripture for this model, for Scripture "does not portray the Church as a single tightly knit society." Yes, as a community of believers we need and have always had some form and order, but this must be secondary to the other models or images of the church. We must resist the temptation to domesticate God. It is good to keep in mind, with Pius XI, that the church is made for us, not we for the church, and that the bishops are not delegates or officiants of the pope and do not act in his name.

The Vatican II document on the church calls it the house of God, the household of God, our Mother, spouse, the kingdom of Christ now present in mystery, a sheepfold, the field of God, the flock of Christ, the edifice of God (of which we are living stones [1 Pt 2:5]), the New Jerusalem, the people of God. Reflecting on the many images of the church should make us hesitant about leaving.

We might also recall that "when St. Paul applies the expression of Body of Christ to the Church, he means the one body which gathers together within it, in the Spirit, the whole assembly of believers by means of the sacraments, and principally the Eucharist" (Marie-Joseph le Guillou in Rahner, ed., *Encyclopedia of Theology*).

Many of Jesus' disciples "broke away and would not remain in his company any longer." When Jesus asked the Twelve if they also wanted to leave him, Peter gave an answer that we could ponder, "Lord, to whom can we go?" (Jn 6:68)

We remember that it was God who called us together in Christ and God who unites us in one body through the Spirit. Born Catholics, bored with their own mediocrity and thus not active in the church, might be spiritually rejuvenated by meditating on the Rite of Christian Initiation of Adults. It could give them a sense of who they are as Catholics.

Some people leave the church because it is a church of sinners. It reminds me of the old story of the man who refused to join because there were too many hypocrites in the church. "Come on in," said the preacher. "We've always got room for one more." St. Augustine said that the whole church cries, "Forgive us our sins!"

"She is blemished and wrinkled," he said. "But through contrition these blemishes are removed, these wrinkles smoothed away. The Church's unceasing prayer is one of contrition that she may be made pure. And so it will remain until the end of time."

If when we contemplate marriage, we look for a perfect spouse, forget it. If we look for a perfect church, forget it. Christ is still with it and puts up with it. To us he says, "I have chosen you." That's enough.

I still have a difficult time convincing laypeople that they *are* the church. With the pastors they are responsible for building up the church. Rather than folding their tents and silently stealing away, they should speak up. "The body of the faithful as a whole," says the constitution on the church, "anointed as they are by the Holy One, cannot err in matters of belief."

The theologians of the Middle Ages never composed a treatise on the church, so I won't attempt it either— though this could go on for ten thousand pages more. As I said, a tough question.

Leave? No. Better to imitate Euphrasia. When the church of St. Sofia was being built she, a destitute widow, drew from her mattress a wisp of straw and gave it to the oxen that drew the marble from the ships.

Reflection Questions

- Do you—or have you ever—considered yourself "outside the church?" What brought you to that place? When you came back, what brought you back?

- Is there anything you miss about the way the church used to be? What does this represent for you?

- What does it mean for you to be a Catholic? How has this answer changed for you over the years?

- Fr. Fehren, at the conclusion of this chapter, argues that the church is a church of sinners. What do you think about that?

THIRTEEN

Double Trouble

"Jesus loves me, this I know, 'cause the Bible tells me so." And now my bank loves me too, so I have the best of both worlds.

You see, I received this nice letter from the vice president of the bank. And even though it is one of the largest banks in the country he even knew my name. He explained that some of those nasty competitive banks might be charging their customers "unexpected charges." But for me, my bank "created a new, simplified checking service" which would make my checking "more valuable than ever."

This vice president is, oh, just ever so nice. And why is he doing this for me? No, not because he is paid hundreds of thousands of dollars yearly in salary. He is making my checking "more valuable than ever before" because he "believes that you (me!) should enjoy complete freedom and convenience in your (my!) banking." How generous and thoughtful of him. His place in heaven will be near the top.

And he is grateful to me. "It's our way of saying thank you for banking" with them. I am drooling in his gracious affection.

But.

But what?

I feel almost guilty for letting a slight suspicion enter my mind, lulled by verbal solicitude. What was "new," "valuable," or "better" in my checking account? Nothing. Nothing changed. Yes, I would get "free" checks, but I don't use a million a month. I could get "unlimited certified checks"—needed once in ten years. And "stop payments" on checks—again, needed once in ten years. That's it.

Oh, only one more thing: this ever-loving bank would now charge me $186 a year whether I used my checking account or not. I had no choice.

George Orwell, where are you when I need you? Orwell, readers will recall, in 1948 wrote a novel of the future State, a country ruled by Big Brother. Thought control is absolute and the national language is Newspeak. The novel, *1984*, was made into a movie even more depressing than the novel.

Newspeak, according to one expert, "is language that makes the bad seem good, the negative appear positive, the unpleasant appear attractive. It avoids or shifts responsibility and is at variance with its real or purported meaning." It limits or diminishes thought. Advertisers and politicians use it unashamedly. I have known one stockbroker for years; try as I may I can never get a straight answer out of her. You can lose $10,000 when the market goes down the and stockbroker will merely call it a "correction." Newspeak.

The military are experts at Newspeak. In the Vietnamese war, some thought that we had to destroy the country in order to save it. A Vietnam vet told me that he was there a year before he realized that when officers referred to "indigenous personnel" they meant the local people.

Nineteen-eighty-four has come and gone, and George Orwell, who died in 1950, would not be surprised that Newspeak has to a great extent become our unofficial language. It is everywhere.

Even in the church?

It is a question to be considered, for we sense that Newspeak is a form of dishonesty; it is misleading and it avoids facts. It is an escape from responsibility. It is so pervasive in our language, so accepted and sometimes so subtle or deceptive, that it could creep into our practice of the faith and into our prayer life. Our sins could be considered virtues and our sins of omission untroubling.

Paul asks the Corinthians, "Do I make my plans according to ordinary human standards, ready to say 'Yes, yes' and 'No, no' at the same time?" (2 Cor 1:17) No Newspeak for him. James also advises against it: "Let your 'Yes' be yes and your 'No' be no" (5:12).

Yes, they were echoing Jesus: "Let your word be 'Yes, Yes' or 'No, No'; anything more than this comes from the evil one" (Mt 5:37). If God is honest with us, can we always be honest with God? It is difficult for us to be honest with each other. The Greek Cynic philosopher Diogenes (d. 324 B.C.) is pictured with a lantern out looking for a true or honest person. As I write this, the monster ruling Iraq calls hostages his "guests" and after taking Kuwait by force says he "is looking for a peaceful solution." Thus, bank robbers can freely keep their loot if they "look for a peaceful solution."

Are we tempted to use Newspeak and doublethink with God? I didn't think much about it until an editor wrote asking if we "can have an honest relationship with God." Do we try to hide from God as Adam and Eve did? Perhaps, I don't know, one contributing factor to the decline in the practice of sacramental confession was a lack of candor on the part of some penitents in confessing to God. Of what value is a dishonest confession? May as well skip it.

The Lord's Prayer is the most frequent of prayers but also, I think, one of the most difficult prayers. Do we always mean what we say when we pray, "Thy will be done"? If we really mean that, then many other prayers could be superfluous. I know Catholics who refuse to speak to each other. I presume that they pray the Our Father, at least at Mass. In effect, they are telling God not to forgive them, for they say, "Forgive us our trespasses *as we forgive those who trespass against us.*" Are we using Newspeak, saying what we do not mean? After giving this prayer, Christ wanted to make clear what we are praying, for he added, "If you do not forgive others, neither will your Father forgive your trespasses" (Mt 6:15). This is repeated in Mark 11:25.

One bishop kneels before abortion clinics and recites prayers. But I don't see him praying in front of movie and TV studios. Even if sex is not necessary to story development, producers seem to throw it in whenever possible. I'm not opposed to sex, or I wouldn't be here. God created it, so it is good. But again and again and again in movies and TV shows people not married to each other hop in the sack and they do so without any notion that a child might result; they do so without any sense of responsibility. Our young people grow up seeing this and it seems the normal thing to do.

Then they become pregnant and "pro-lifers" worry about abortion. It's like closing the barn door after horse is gone. There seems to be lots of Newspeak in the abortion debate.

One state governor, a Catholic, was invited to speak on abortion and the law at a Catholic parish. Before he could begin his talk, a lawyer, not a member of the parish, challenged him on something. The pastor was going to invite the intruder out but the governor said, "No, let me talk to him."

"You believe that every abortion from the moment of conception is murder?" asked the governor.

"Yes," was the emphatic answer.

"And you want that written into the United States Constitution?"

Again the answer was yes.

"And the penalty for murder is execution or life imprisonment?"

The lawyer raised his voice with "Absolutely, yes!"

Every ear was listening. The governor, who was standing in the aisle with the "pro-lifer," pointed to a fifteen-year-old girl seated next to the aisle. "If she had an abortion," asked the governor, "you would have her executed or sent to prison for life?" The lawyer silently left. The governor had no time for Newspeak in a very complicated matter.

If we use or even try drugs we have blood on our hands—even marijuana, under any of its popular names. "It is harmless," I hear people say, "It doesn't hurt me." But its journey here is a trail of blood. If I buy it I am responsible for the killing and corruption because I pay for it. Here "harmless" is a Newspeak word. If a drug does not harm me physically, it certainly harms me morally.

From our pockets comes the money to kill priests, nuns, church catechists, and other lay people in El Salvador. We pay the military and supply the weapons. The *New York Times* once referred to "one of the most brutal crackdowns on religious workers in Latin America." Our "macho" presidents with typical political doubletalk called it a democracy.

We also hear of the increase in street attacks on gays by cowardly young gangs. It may be traceable in part, said one spokesperson, "to inaction from public officials and church leaders." When gays are denied church property for meetings or Mass, for gathering in the name of the Lord, it is always with some "we-love-you-but" Newspeak and likewise when church officials crusade to deny them civil rights.

I would have loved to hear the doubletalk when a pope conferred the papal title of Countess on Annie Leary. She lived in a grand mansion, was a big spender, loved gilt-framed mirrors, of which she had sixty-eight, and gave spectacular parties. Imagine Jesus giving papal court titles.

A parish council, trusting in the Vatican II documents on the laity, voted to endorse the call for reform in the Catholic church. The parish council does not have the right to speak in the name of the parish, said the local bishop. The action was neither "official" nor "appropriate." Only the pastor or the bishop may speak in the name of the parish, he added. Forget the beautiful things said about the laity in the documents on the laity and on the church. It was nothing but Newspeak, you laity; get back into your place at the bottom and shut up.

"Magisterium" is another ill-used word. Theologians who teach are to swear loyalty to it and others are to "suffer for the truth in silence." In effect, the magisterium is one person (he appoints others who agree with him). But Dom Bede Griffiths, O.S.B., says that the magisterium consists of four organs: (1) the pope and the curia; (2) the bishops; (3) the theologians; and (4) most important, the laity, who through the gift of the Holy Spirit in baptism share in the authority of Christ as prophet, priest and king. "All alike share in the magisterium, or the teaching authority of the Church."

I'm not sure if I am getting any point across but I am uneasy and I sometimes wonder if the malaise some feel in the church today and the exodus of Catholics from church practice isn't caused at least in part by the doubletalk or Newspeak we hear in the church.

"My teacher, let me *see*," prayed the blind man (Mk 10:51; emphasis added). Perhaps we should join his prayer so that Christ can say to us, "Blessed are your eyes, for they *see*" (Mt 13:16; emphasis added).

Reflection Questions

- Go through the Lord's Prayer phrase by phrase. Which parts present no problems for you? Which phrases are more difficult? Reflect on the difficult parts.

- Fr. Fehren suggests that we should focus more attention on casual sex in TV and movies than on abortion. Do you agree? Why or why not?

- Fr. Fehren talks about people who claim marijuana is a "harmless" drug. What do you think about this?

- Fr. Fehren quotes one spokesperson who suggests that gay-bashing is the result of "inaction by public officials and church leaders?" Is this fair? Should the church allow Catholic gay people to use church property for meetings or Mass?

- Fr. Fehren suggests the magisterium of the church includes the pope and curia, the bishops, theologians, and the laity. Are one of these groups more responsible than others for "Newspeak?" Do the laity in any sense contribute to Newspeak?

- What is your favorite example of Newspeak?

FOURTEEN

A Night at the Opera

Opera, anyone? Oh, not just any ol' opera. Maybe an opera by a Jew about two other Jews? An opera, in fact, by a composer whose music had been described for thirty years and more as "empty ingenuity and ingenious pedantry...fanciful imaginings of a lunatic...drunken gesture of a drunken professor."

The music is twelve-tone atonality. Is that nonsense or just an oxymoron (like is a moronic ox an oxymoron?). There is also "bewildering ugly dissonance," which "has tortured the music out of shape."

Not only that, it is labeled an "opera in three acts," yet it has only two acts. And the cost of a good seat is $55. Ouch. You going? I remind you that the cost of the libretto in print so tiny that it is almost unreadable is $6. Thirteen small pages. I'm not going.

Yes, I am going. Why am I going? The prognostications are not good. Yet I will borrow the $55 from my Indigent Clergy Fund (of which I am the sole beneficiary) and go. Why?

Because it is a big, wide, wonderful world and God invites us to experience all we can. God didn't make things just for the heck of it; God made everything for us. So we had better have a look at it. When I was a college teacher I used to tell my students to go everywhere, see everything, try eating everything, read everything, meet everyone and do almost everything (restrained by morality).

I have just returned from Uttar Pradesh (northern India) and Nepal. In January I am going to Antarctica. "Why on earth are you going there?" friends ask in unbelief. Because it's there, I answer, and because God created it and God might be offended if no one bothered to see what God had made for us.

Likewise with things that we co-create with God. We are made to the image and likeness of God, and God is a creator so we also must be creators. God's creation is old (and we are doing our best to destroy it), but God helps us create new things. God helped Arnold Schoenberg create an off-beat opera, *Moses und Aron*.

So I thought that I had better check it out. By being willing to take a chance on something new and unknown, we may learn something and we may enjoy something and experience some pleasure that our timidity or lack of curiosity may have denied us. God expects us to use the intellect God gave us.

"It's not over," said someone, "till the fat lady sings." I knew, however, that *Moses und Aron* would have no bosomy sopranos, no corpulent contraltos, no tubby tenors, no pot-bellied basses. But the theme of the opera is biblical, and that was my second reason for going.

There are other Bible-oriented operas: Boito's *Mefistofele*, in which the devil has a discourse with God in the Prologue; Saint-Saens' *Samson and Delila* and Richard Strauss' *Salome*, both highly theatrical; and Menotti's lighter *Amahl and the Night Visitors*, popular at Christmas since the night visitors are the Three Kings.

So I go. I can always walk out at the intermission. The stage setting at the New York City Opera is a nearly empty space flanked on three sides by flat, plain, sand-colored walls. Except for a few props of the same color, the stage is bare. Sand and empty space: the desert.

The desert, where a collection of primitive, Semitic tribes became the People of God. The desert, where Jesus confronted Satan. The desert, where in the novel and movie *True Confessions*, a worldly priest finds peace with God. The desert each one of us experiences, where there is no place to hide from God.

Omygawd, the people on stage are all one color, a mustard color, hair, faces, skirts, pants, jackets, hands. Will monochrome and dissonant counterpoint twelve-tone without tonality "music" equal automatic monotony? Much of Schoenberg, says one critic, "is inert and static...an experiment in beauty which destroys beauty and leaves only a shell of ugliness and frustration."

Like anyone else, I have suffered enough ugliness and frustration. Even the orchestra is hidden under a black screen. I had better get out. Too late. I'm in the middle of the row. I'd have to crawl over fifteen people. I'm trapped. As a last resort maybe I can quietly laugh my way through it. I remember the Marx Brothers movie, *A Night at the Opera*.

The lights dim. The opera begins. Thank God I'm trapped. I remember my first reason for coming. I'm here to experience something new. "Anyone who approaches the work with an open mind," the conductor had said in an interview, "has an amazing discovery in the story. You know from the very first minute that you're in the presence of an astonishing creation. The opening chord of the opera is like a new universe, a fantastic voice from another sphere."

He's right. "God writes straight with crooked lines," according to a French author. Or, as an old Protestant hymn has it, "God works in mysterious ways his wonders to perform." Anyhow, I'll give God credit and thanks for getting me here, for my second reason for coming—that the opera is based on the Bible—is amply fulfilled.

We recall from the book of Exodus the story of Moses and his brother Aaron. When God called Moses to lead his people out of the slavery of Egypt to the land flowing with milk and honey, Moses objected that the people might not believe him or listen to his plea. So God gave him two signs to work: Moses could turn his rod into a snake and back into a rod again and his hand could turn leprous and be healthy again.

But Moses still would not accept the mission: "O my Lord, I have never been eloquent, neither in the past nor even now that you have spoken to your servant; but I am slow of speech and slow of tongue" (4:10). So God promises to assist him in speaking and will teach him what to say.

But Moses insists, "O my Lord, please send someone else" (4:13). By now God is peeved, but God gives in and says that Moses' brother Aaron can assist him and be the spokesman. This account can stimulate us to examine ourselves on how well we respond to God's call, to see if we make excuses for not accepting our mission from God.

The work assigned may not be easy. In Schoenberg's operatic interpretation, Moses is slow of tongue and speech because he does not know how to communicate his faith in God and his experience of God. The opening words of the opera are by Moses: "Only one, infinite, thou omnipresent one, unperceived and inconceivable God!"

He understands, as far as it is possible, the nature of God, but how does one get this across to people—how express the inexpressible? Jesus tried to teach us about God, but most of us do not fully believe him. Someone has said that the only thing we know about God is that we know nothing about God.

Every preacher has the problem of trying to communicate God to people. Writers on religion rack their brains in the effort. Parents suffer when they cannot transmit their faith to their children. Religion teachers wonder how effective their methods are. Even when we want to enlighten friends we often feel impotent and thus simply avoid the subject of God.

Today we hear much of evangelization, a cumbersome word, but the problem is the same as Moses had—how do we impart God's message? At the end of the opera Moses is alone on the stage "speak-singing," "O word, thou word, that I lack!"

In due time, "the Word became flesh and lived among us" (Jn 1:14). Even then "the world did not know him" and "his own people did not accept him" (Jn 1:10,11). But those who did accept him were empowered to become children of God; they saw his glory, the glory of the Son filled with enduring love; they received a share in his fullness (Jn 1:12,14,16).

"No one has ever seen God," says John. "It is God the only Son, who is close to the Father's heart, who has made him known" (1:18). Jesus, however, also had his problems in revealing the Father. "Do you not understand this parable?" he asks the Twelve (Mk 4:13). "Have you still no faith?" (Mk 4:40). "Do you still not perceive or understand?" Jesus asked the disciples. "Are your hearts hardened? Do you have eyes, and fail to see? Do you have ears, and fail to hear?" (Mk 8:17-18)

When Jesus spoke of himself as life-giving food, "many of his disciples turned back and no longer went about with him" (Jn 6:66). He wept over the city of Jerusalem, saying, "If you, even you, had only recognized on this day the things that make for peace!" (Lk 19:42) Are we in that city?

We have elements of both Moses and Aaron in us, contemplative and earthy, for we are made of body and spirit. We are not disembodied spirits; we are not angels. The flesh is good, for "Jesus Christ has come in the flesh" (1 Jn 4:2). We use material things in our worship and in the sacraments: "unless you eat the flesh of the Son of Man and drink his blood" (Jn 6:53). We need sacred pictures, statues and crucifixes in our homes, churches, schools.

The mistake is to let Aaron dominate and be too busy to meditate and to pray. "Purify your thinking," says Moses in the opera. And a youth sings, "Annihilate this image of the temporal; clear be the view of eternity!" The people, however, want a god that they can see and touch. So while Moses is up on the mountain in communion with God, Aaron makes the golden calf for the people to worship. (Is there a golden calf in our lives?)

Daniel, who worshiped the "living God," destroyed the "great dragon" the Babylonians worshiped (14:23-27). We search our own lives to see if it is a *who* or a *what* that we worship. Moses "saw that the people were running wild" (Ex 32:25). Jesus did work miracles, gave signs, but he wanted people to get beyond that. "And he sighed deeply in his spirit and said, 'Why does this generation ask for a sign? Truly I tell you, no sign will be given to this generation" (Mk 8:12)

How will we tell people about God? First, and at least, by our lives. Like Enoch and Abraham we walk with God (Gn 5:24; 24:40). *Be* a letter from Christ. "You are a letter of Christ," says Paul, "...written not with ink but with the Spirit of the living God, not on tablets of stone but on tablets of human hearts" (2 Cor 3:3).

If we follow in Christ's footsteps (Mt 10:38 and elsewhere), someone may follow us.

The opera house was full. No one left at the intermission.

Reflection Questions

- Do you buy the author's philosophy of life: Go everywhere, see everything, meet everyone, do everything?

- "God writes straight with crooked lines." Do you have a favorite episode from your life that illustrates this wisdom?

- When have you resisted God's call? What was the source of your resistance?

- When have you identified with Moses' inability to describe God? Did you give up and "simply avoid the subject of God" or did you continue?

- What is the best way for you to tell people about God?

FIFTEEN

Henry and Teresa

"**A**s far back as I can remember, I've always wanted to be a gangster." These are the words and the dream of Henry Hill, an adolescent in the movie *Goodfellas*.

I want to be a saint, said another adolescent, Teresa Martin. "The good God would not inspire unattainable desires, so I may, in spite of my littleness, aspire to holiness."

Both fulfilled their dreams.

One yearned and planned and schemed to become a hood. He wanted the money, the cars, the power that the local mobsters had. He saw that they could get frilly gun molls to kowtow to them and service them. He saw the snazzy suits they wore. He wanted all that.

So he worked his way up in the local mob. He began by running errands for the members. He showed the proper respect and was deferential to them. Observing due modesty, he played his cards right until he was fully accepted, and beatings, extortion terror, robbery and killing became his way of life. He was successful.

No, this was not the bigtime mafia. It was a local, neighborhood operation. He was determined, but his ambitions were not considered excessive. Teresa, also, was determined and her place for achieving her goal was also nearby, the Carmelite convent in Lisieux. Her resolve to join the convent was so strong that she went to Rome to ask the pope himself for permission to join at the early age of fifteen. The convent had refused her because of her youth.

After a papal Mass, in those days, pilgrims were allowed to come up to the pope and kiss his white slipper. They were forbidden to speak to him, but Teresa, resolute in her belief that the convent was the place for her to become a saint, broke the rule and asked for his permission to enter the convent. "Holy Father, if you said yes, everyone else would be willing." He blessed her and said, "You will enter if it is God's will."

It was not Teresa's ambition to become a canonized saint; such pride would have destroyed her sanctity. She just wanted to become holy, to be like Jesus, whom she loved. And she thought that the convent was the best place for her to achieve that. There are as many ways to sanctity as there are people, and for Teresa the convent was the way. The important thing is that though she was a teenager, she was concerned about holiness.

Religious orders and seminaries these days are leery about accepting people under twenty-one — perhaps because so many religious and clergy have left to find "fulfillment" elsewhere. Just before he became a teenager, Jesus showed his intention of doing his Father's will (which is the essence of holiness) when at the age of twelve he remained in the temple in Jerusalem. He explained to Mary and Joseph that he had to be about his Father's business (or in his Father's "house").

He was not too young to follow the way of holiness. Indeed, Luke says that as Jesus grew in size he grew also in wisdom and grace (2:40).

By contrast, this headline once ran across the top of a full-page advertisement in the *New York Times*: "When I grow up I want to be a junkie." Below that was a picture of a young girl. Below this picture the text said, "Sure it sounds ridiculous. After all, nobody ever makes plans to become a drug addict. But that doesn't stop it from happening. In fact, one out of every two kids has used drugs." Then there was a plea to parents, asking them to help protect their children, especially by setting an example.

Teresa's parents and grandparents did set a good example; they were saintly people. Her father is considered a saint worthy of canonization.

In an Off-Broadway play, *Handy Dandy*, an activist nun asks the judge, who has sentenced her to a short prison term for trespassing in a peace protest, what his aim in life is. "To get through life without pain," he answers.

That ambition, or lack of it, is not evil, but it is not enough if we wish to help young people become holy as God calls them to be. The judge's escapist intention may seem like a comfortable, neutral plan, but Christ says that there is no neutral ground. "Whoever is not with me is against me," says Jesus, "and whoever does not gather with me scatters" (Mt 12:30; Lk 11:23).

Can we expect children to want holiness if the parents are lukewarm? Can we expect them to "strive first for the kingdom of God" (Mt 6:33) if we encourage laying up earthly treasure (though good in itself) as their life purpose instead of the "imperishable" wreath (1 Cor 9:25)?

The name is fictitious, but Henry Hill is a real person, as are the others in the movie. He testified against his fellow gangsters and is now in the government witness protection program. He has not repented. His imprisoned buddies, I hear, know where he is hiding and expect to kill him when they get out.

His gifts to others were beatings, bullets, and robbery. Teresa's gifts to the cloistered Sisters she lived with were love, patience, concern, kindness and humility. Even after death her gift was "a shower of roses," as she had planned, helping those who called on her.

She did not leave the convent; she died there in 1887 and in 1925 was declared a saint. She did not, however, slide slipshod into holiness. She said that she preferred an elevator, but knowing that this was impossible, she planned her "little way" to holiness. We put a lot of planning into reaching our earthly goals; how much more important it is to have a plan for attaining our ultimate goal, that of being holy so that we may be welcomed into God's heavenly kingdom.

One poll reported that nine out of ten Americans say that they have never doubted the existence of God, eight of ten believe in a Judgment Day, seven of ten believe in life after death, and four of ten attend church in a typical week. On the same page that this poll appeared, there was a news item reporting that in the previous six months murders in the United States had increased eight percent (twenty percent in large cities). Likewise with other violent crimes. If we have God, why do we need drugs?

I am not sure how to reconcile the two reports, but we can see that riding loose in a religious saddle is not the way to the perfection to which God calls us. God chose us, says St. Paul, "to be holy and blameless before him in love" (Eph 1:4).

There are too many biblical references to our call to holiness to list here, but note Zachary, "filled with the Holy Spirit" (Lk 1:67) when he recovered his speech on naming his son John: "...that we...might serve him [God] without fear, in holiness and righteousness before him all our days" (Lk 1:74-75).

In the Old Testament, the central idea of the book of Leviticus is that "you shall be holy, for I am holy" (11:45). The first epistle of Peter recalls this, saying, "As he who called you is holy, be holy yourselves in all your conduct" (1:15).

We won't become holy, however, unless we have our mind set on it. St. Scholastica said that we must will to be a saint. That is a beginning. At least, we must be willing to become saints. We can say now what Christ said on the cross, "Father, into your hands I commend my spirit" (Lk 23:46). We can become saints only by choice.

"My desire is to depart and be with Christ, for that is far better," said Paul (Phil 1:23). But, someone asked me, *how* do we get to heaven? I felt like answering as one person did when he was asked how to get to Carnegie Hall: "Practice, practice, practice."

Founders of religious orders usually wrote instructions to help their members in their efforts toward perfection. St. Ignatius wrote the *Spiritual Exercises* for the Jesuits. St. Benedict wrote the *Holy Rule* for his monks. There are seventy-three chapters, yet he calls it a "little rule for beginners." We will not let rules overcome the Spirit, but we do need guidance, planning, specifics, or we will just float along aimlessly. Jesus didn't just tell us to love, he told us how to love and he set an example.

We can make our own "holy rule" for our own particular life. "Train yourself in godliness," says Paul, "for, while physical training is of some value, godliness is valuable in every way, holding promise for both the present life and the life to come" (1 Tim 4:7-8).

More than a century ago an anonymous person made up this brief rule for himself:

> Live as in the sight of God. This is what
> Abraham did: "The Lord, in whose presence I
> have always walked..." (Gn 24:40). This is
> what Enoch did: "Enoch walked with God"
> (Gn 5:24).
>
> Do nothing you would not like God to see:
> "The fact is that whether you eat or
> drink—whatever you do—you should do all
> for the glory of God" (1 Cor 10:31).
>
> Say nothing you would not like God to
> hear: "O Lord, set a watch before my mouth, a
> guard at the door of my lips" (Ps 141:3).

Sing nothing that will not be melodious to God's ear: "Sing praise to the Lord with all your hearts" (Eph 5:19).

Write nothing you would not like God to read: "O Lord, you understand my thoughts from afar" (Ps 139:2).

Go no place you would not like God to find you: "My journeys and my rest you scrutinize" (Ps 139:3).

Read no book of which you would not like God to say, "Show it to me": "Turn away my eyes from seeing what is vain" (Ps 119:37).

Henry and Teresa. Both chose, and then they devised a plan for their lives. Henry now lives in hiding and fears for his life. Teresa is enjoying the happiness of heaven. The choice is ours. If we choose to accept God's call to holiness, we must chart the way. Haphazard won't do.

Reflection Questions

- How do you answer the peace activist's question, "What is your aim in life?"

- The author suggests that our aim should be to become holy. Are you comfortable with this goal? What does "becoming holy" mean in this day and age?

- What obstacles stand in the way of your effort to become holy?

Sixteen

For Sale:
One Hair Shirt

To read or see Shakespeare's play *Othello* is, among other things, to follow the trail of a handkerchief. For thereby, on that slight piece of cloth, hangs a tale. An Egyptian gave it to Othello's mother; she on her deathbed gave it to Othello; he gives it to his wife, Desdemona; she misplaces it, and it is found by Emilia; she gives it to Iago; he gives it to Cassio, and Cassio gives it to Bianca, his lowbrow mistress. It all ends, to be technical, in uxorcide: a jealous husband, who "loved not wisely but too well," kills his wife.

I thought of that hanky's journey when I read the hair shirt episode in J. F. Powers' superb novel, *Wheat That Springeth Green*. A friend of a seminary rector gives him a hair shirt "as a joke." The rector gives it to a seminarian leaving for the Trappists. He, in turn, gives it to Joe, another seminarian and the protagonist of the novel.

Joe starts wearing it (he washes it out every night) and then the rector wants it back. He then changes his mind, after a heart attack, and says that Joe can keep it. Joe is to use his own judgment about wearing it. He wears it for some time further but decides that it is foolish to bypass humanity and yet try to get in touch with God directly by the hair shirt and other ascetical practices.

Hold on, Father, what's a hair shirt? And where do you get them? In fur shops? And why is a hair shirt?

A hair shirt, as the ascetical cognoscenti of bygone days would know, is a sleeveless garment, something like a vest, made of coarse animal hair and worn next to the skin. It's not just irritating; it's agony. Wearing it was a means of doing penance for one's sins (though anyone zealous enough to wear one probably had very few sins to atone for).

Not being in the market for one anymore, I do not know where they can be obtained today. Forty years ago they were available from a Carmelite monastery in Canada. From the same place one could send for a girdle or belt made of pieces of stiff wire so woven that sharp ends of wire encircled one's waistline and pressed against the flesh.

Why would anyone wear a prickly undergarment or a barbed belt? Is there such a thing as holy masochism? In porno movies, someone may get an erotic charge by being whipped, but some saints scourged themselves. I believe it was call "the discipline." Why did Christians ardent for holiness use these and other means of self-punishment? I have a saintly friend (even when he was in high school I sensed his holiness), a Trappist in Peru, who sleeps on a board and fasts stringently. Why this self-denial, mortification, austerity, penance, fasting?

Don't we have enough grief, hardship and suffering without voluntarily adding on more? Don't we have enough pain, unsought and unwanted, without inflicting more ourselves? Is God a sadist egging us on to more self-torture? St. Peter Damian, for example, was tormented by headaches, yet he added other forms of self-denial, including fasting and the scourge. Does God require this? What does God get out of it?

God, obviously, does not need anything. He does ask for love of God and neighbor, but that is for our good. Whatever we do "for" God we are ultimately doing for ourselves. If that is selfish, that is O.K., for we must love ourselves (Mt 22:39). Maybe Jesus can help answer our questions. We see that he himself fasted for forty days and forty nights (Mt 4:2).

So there is the best example. But what was the situation when Jesus fasted? We note two things. He was preparing for the beginning of his public life. He was girding up, as it were, for the battle, getting into shape spiritually. It may be fitting to call it boot camp, that stay in the desert, but Jesus was preparing for the work ahead and evidently prayer and fasting were useful for that purpose.

We note secondly that his first confrontation was with the devil. Fortified with the prayer and fasting, Jesus vanquished the devil and his temptations. A runner in the New York Marathon told me of his strenuous training for the race. He was one of 25,000 who happily subjected their bodies to punishment so rigorous that a desert anchorite might envy the zeal.

"Athletes exercise self-control in all things," says Paul. "They do it to receive a perishable wreath, but we an imperishable one. I punish my body and enslave it, so that after proclaiming to others I myself should not be disqualified" (1 Cor 9:25,27).

Jesus was following the example of Moses, who stayed on the mountain "with the LORD forty days and forty nights; he neither ate bread nor drank water" (Ex 34:28). Moses then went down to instruct the people and lead them to the promised Land.

Thus we see that the tradition of fasting is ancient. There are other examples in the Old Testament. Sometimes the fasting is done in penitence, as in the case of Daniel: "Then I turned to the Lord God, to seek an answer by prayer and supplication with fasting and sackcloth and ashes" (9:3). David fasted in petition for the life of his child. Fasting was also a sign of mourning. Cultic laws did not command fasting, but sometimes a public fast was declared. Jesus didn't mandate fasting, but he supposes that his disciples will fast, for he cautions them not to do it to show off their piety:

> And whenever you fast, do not look dismal, like the hypocrites, for they disfigure their faces so as to show others that they are fasting. Truly I tell you, they have received their reward. But when you fast, put oil on your head and wash your face, so that your fasting may be seen not by others but by your Father who is in secret; and your Father who sees in secret will reward you (Mt 6:16-18).

In the early church, when certain "prophets and teachers...were worshiping the Lord and fasting," the Holy Spirit came upon them and told them to set apart Barnabas and Saul for apostolic work. So they prayed and fasted some more and then imposed hands on the two and sent them off on their mission (Acts 13:1-3).

Fasting was nearly always accompanied by prayer. That separates it from mere dieting (though dieters usually pray to lose a few pounds). Hair shirts and piercing metal belts are out of style today (that's why mine are up for sale), and fasting, though a practice in the church since its beginning, has fallen on hard times.

The laws of fasting and/or abstinence gradually fell into disuse in the past fifty years or so—perhaps because the self-denial was *legislated*. The law can kill, as we know, and the Spirit can give life. Among the three traditional practices of Lent, prayer and almsgiving are more emphasized these days than the fasting and abstinence. That is a healthful trend, for I can remember serious discussion about whether a malted milk broke the fast or not. Etcetera. Even the eucharistic fast provided grist for legalistic minds. "Is it a sin to smoke before receiving Holy Communion?"

Misguided, nitpicking, egotistic or narcissistic asceticism can become a substitute for love. True self-denial or ascetical practices are based on love or they have no value. Ask St. Paul: "If I give away all my possessions, and if I hand over my body so that I may boast, but do not have love, I gain nothing" (1 Cor 13:3).

"Why do we fast, but you do not see? Why humble ourselves, but you do not notice?" the people ask God in Isaiah 58:3. God says that their fasting is useless because it ends in quarreling. In the rest of this beautiful chapter, God speaks of the works of mercy as the best fasting.

The braggart Pharisee fasted, but Jesus said that he was not justified (Lk 18:14). Fasting based on love is very beneficial.

> Yet even now, says the LORD,
>   return to me with all your heart,
> with fasting, with weeping, and with mourning....
> Blow the trumpet in Zion;
>   sanctify a fast (Jl 2:12,15).

We may say that we have enough grief and hardship and pain without voluntarily taking on anymore. A wife may consider her nagging husband her hair shirt; a husband may consider his alcoholic wife a hair shirt; parents may consider their culturally alienated children their hair shirt.

Fasting, obviously, is not urged on the starving. But over the many centuries in which asceticism in various forms was recommended and practiced, life was never easy. Most of the people who fasted, for instance, were not living in palaces. Life was tough then, as it is now. When St. Patrick, a teenager, was captured by barbarians and was forced to tend cattle, he suffered from hunger and cold. Yet he prayed and fasted. Doing so, he grew stronger in faith and love.

In Matthew and Mark, Jesus says that if anyone would come after him he should deny himself and take up his cross and follow Jesus, but in Luke those who would follow him are asked to take up the cross *daily* — a call to asceticism. Fasting helps us to "set [our] minds on things that are above, not on things that are on earth" (Col 3:2). Fasting can help clarify our vision and keep us from being "set on earthly things" or making our belly our god (Phil 3:19). It helps us to empty ourselves in more ways than one so that we can be filled with Christ.

Bodily fasting can help us to see the value of fasting from material goods, to see that rust and moth will consume them, to see that we have here no lasting city. Where our heart is, there our treasure will be. This does not mean that we despise the goods God has made for us. We will not succeed in loving God more just because we love creatures less, according to St. Thomas Aquinas. We do not give glory to God by disdaining his creation.

But fasting, of many kinds, can help prevent lukewarmness and flabbiness in our spiritual life. If we find ourselves sliding further from God, we can take charge of ourselves again by devising or setting up, as founders of religious orders did for their members, a Holy Rule for ourselves.

We cannot embrace Christ without the cross he freely accepted.

Reflection Questions

- Is there a place for fasting—or other forms of self-denial—in your life?

- Where are the "hair shirts" in your life?

- Do you recall an example of self-discipline from your life that seemed to go too far? Do you recall an episode that seemed "right?" What was the difference?

SEVENTEEN

The Man in the Santa Claus Suit

Mulled cider, egg nog, vintage wines, exotic Moroccan food, rich cinnamon ice cream, Christmas cookies, hot Ethiopian coffee, V.S.O.P. cognac, a twinkling, real, not plastic, Christmas tree with old-fashioned decorations, an elegant spacious apartment overlooking the lordly Hudson River, a small group of smartly dressed, well-traveled bright interesting people.

I had just been part of that scene.

When I left to take a sidestreet to the subway, it was dark outside and it was raining. Opening my foldup umbrella, I noticed on the otherwise deserted street a figure shuffling toward me. As he came closer, I saw that he was dressed in a Santa Claus suit. It was two days before Christmas and Jolly Ol' St. Nick did not look so jolly.

I am not turning this incident into a sentimental Christmas story, but the warm glow I had from the pleasant social gathering began to dissipate and a touch of sadness crept in. Without an umbrella and somewhat soggy, the man had probably donned the garb for a job in which he was used to garner business or to induce donations. Now he reminded me of the pathetic Charlie Chaplin clown.

My spirits brightened a little as I got into a new, well-lit subway car. Plenty of people here. Yet, I realized, they are all strangers. Still, on my way home I could not get that solitary figure out of my mind.

I entered my silent apartment—I am the sole occupant—and the brief sidewalk incident remained with me. I wondered why it bothered me. Was there some significance in that forlorn being clothed in an ill-fitting, silly costume? Our eyes had met for a moment; his were expressionless.

Loneliness, that was it. I realized that the person was a picture of loneliness, the loneliness that we all experience—and suffer.

Because we know the pain of loneliness, we usually are moved to pity or at least sympathy when we see an obviously lonely person. "Sad" and "lonely" are two words that go together.

"Loneliness," wrote John Milton, "is the first thing which God's eye nam'd not good" (*Tetrachordon*). We recall from the book of Genesis that as God created each thing, God saw that it was "good." After creating Adam, however, "The LORD God said, 'It is not good that the man should be alone'" and then God created Eve "as his partner" (2:18).

"There is only one suffering," wrote the French philosopher Gabriel Marcel, "—that is to be alone." He was not speaking of being alone for a time; he meant the condition of being alone, of having no one. We think of that as the most agonizing torment of hell.

Although God made us social beings, there are times when we do like to be alone. Jesus sometimes went off by himself to pray. When he did, though, he talked to his Father. "It is not I alone...," he told the Pharisees, "but I and the Father who sent me" (Jn 8:16).

If in our loneliness we feel that God has abandoned us, we can say for ourselves what Jesus repeats to the

Pharisees: "The one who sent me is with me; he has not left me alone" (Jn 8:29). Jesus then explains that God has not deserted him because he does what pleases the Father. Nor will we be left alone if we follow the example of Jesus.

We sometimes find ourselves in the position of Yahweh in the prophecy of Isaiah:

> I have trodden the winepress alone,
>> and from the peoples no one was with me....
> I looked, but there was no helper;
>> I stared, but there was no one to sustain me
>> (63:3,5).

Jesus experienced this aloneness, for even though he was surrounded by people they did not understand him; they were not one with him (Jn 10:6). The Pharisees did not grasp what he was trying to tell them; some thought that he was possessed by a devil (Jn 10:19,20). They tried to stone him and attempted to arrest him (Jn 10:31,39).

Even his disciples often did not understand him. On one occasion he asked his disciples, "Then do you also fail to understand?" (Mk 7:18). "Do you still not perceive or understand?" he asked them in exasperation another time. "Are your hearts hardened? Do you have eyes, and fail to see? Do you have ears, and fail to hear?" (Mk 8:17-18)

One of his chosen twelve betrayed him; another denied knowing him. In his hour of crisis in the Garden of Gethsemane, his closest friends fell asleep and then fled, leaving him to face his tormentors alone (Mt 26:56). Jesus had foreseen this, for he had told his disciples, "The hour is coming, indeed it has come, when you will be scattered, each one to his home, and you will leave me alone." And once again he reassures himself and lets the disciples know, "Yet I am not alone because the Father is with me" (Jn 16:32).

There may be times when we too may want to utter Christ's plaint from the cross, "My God, my God, why have you forsaken me?" They are the only words of Jesus on the cross recorded by Matthew and Mark. It was an anguished, searing cry from the heart, but it was not a cry of despair. The words are from Psalm 22:1 and were spoken in Aramaic. Jesus may have prayed and remembered the psalms in Aramaic.

We must take the whole psalm into consideration, for it is a prayer of confidence in God. "Do not be far from me, for trouble is near and there is no one to help" (v 11) prays the psalmist. "Deliver my soul from the sword, my life from the power of the dog" (v 20). The psalm ends with the words,

> ...and I shall live for him.
> Posterity will serve him;
>> future generations will be told about the Lord,
> and proclaim his deliverance to a people yet
>> unborn,
>> saying that he has done it (vv 29-31).

The people to be born, the church, is born from the death and resurrection (not Pentecost) of Christ. Even his last words on the cross, "It is finished" (Jn 19:30), can be seen as a triumphant proclamation that he has faithfully fulfilled his Father's will.

It is well to remember when we are painfully alone that Christ has suffered the same, and we will find comfort in Psalm 22 (and the familiar Psalm 23: "you are with me" [v 4]) when we are excluded, isolated, scorned or rejected.

Rejected. That brings up a second observation about the man in the Santa Claus suit. He was not being himself; he was being Santa Claus. Yet he was not Santa Claus. His real self was hidden behind the costume. Such a situation—where we cannot be our true selves—adds to our loneliness.

We sometimes fear to be ourselves, fear to be the person whom God made us to be, because we fear disapproval or penalties. We my be rejected, spurned, or just brushed aside. In one way or another we hide our true self. Because people did not accept Jesus, they "picked up stones to throw at him," so he "hid himself" (Jn 8:59). He hid himself physically; we have other ways of hiding from others.

Gays and lesbians, for instance, experience this rejection. They are often ridiculed, persecuted, and mistreated by ignorant, stupid or bigoted people, including church leaders. In Catholic Ireland there is a law, though rarely enforced, that homosexuality is to be punished by life imprisonment. Although they are proved to be as loyal and courageous as anyone else, they are, in the United States, expelled from military service. Thus because of prejudice against them, many remain in hiding, "in the closet," for they are afraid to be as God in love made them.

They have experienced the words of Psalm 69, "I am the subject of gossip for those who sit in the gate, and the drunkards make songs about me" (v 12). They may have become outcasts (v 8) and found no sympathy or comforters (v 20), but God spurns them not (v 33). It's a lonely life, but they can take comfort from the words of Jesus, "Anyone who comes to me I will never drive away" (Jn 6:37).

God does not make clones; each person is different, a tribute to God's creativity. If we are to love our neighbor as ourself, we must accept people as they are. This, of course, does not mean excusing anti-social and criminal actions. Religions, races, and cultures battle each other all over the world. It is irrational and totally opposed to the spirit of Jesus.

If Christ's Last Supper prayer that all be one is to be answered, each person must be careful not to build walls and must do everything possible, usually in very small ways, to alleviate loneliness, to break down walls, to heal divisions, and to melt hostility, for what we do to others we do to Christ (Mt 25:31-46). If we hold others in contempt we risk the fires of Gehenna (Mt 5:22).

Better to do as the epistle to the Hebrews suggests: "Do not neglect to show hospitality to strangers, for by doing that some have entertained angels without knowing it" (13:2). The author is referring to the story of Abraham, who lavishly entertained three strangers, not knowing that they were messengers from God (Gn 18). Job did the same (Jb 31:32).

Hebrews also tells us to "remember those who are in prison, as though you were in prison with them; those who are being tortured, as though you yourselves were being tortured" (13:3). All prisoners are not behind iron bars; we may have imprisoned people by our prejudice. We must help set them free. The first freedom is to be free to be oneself.

Reflection Questions

- Think of different times in your life: 1) when you were lonely and sad 2) when you were alone and glad to be by yourself 3) when you felt abandoned by God.

- Have you ever felt lonely in a roomful of people?

- Was there ever a time when you deliberately hid yourself from others? Why?

- When you feel isolated, what do you do to break down the walls between yourself and others?

EIGHTEEN

Floating Islands

There was a camel walking down the street in New York City and near it was a three-year-old child in a white dress, a golden plastic halo, and white, gossamer wings. An ignorant TV news reporter did not seem to know what it was all about, but the *New York Times* had it right. Under a newsphoto of the event: "East Harlem Parade Celebrates the Epiphany."

As usual, I am not sure how to say what I want to say since I am not sure of exactly what I want to say. But I think that something should be said so that we can reflect on it, think about it, get some answers and maybe find some guidance.

O.K., HF, stop stalling. What's the problem?

The Epiphany photo got me to thinking or puzzling about what we have lost in the church and what we have let go, what should be discarded and what should be saved, and whether we can do anything about it or not. What is the cockle and what is the wheat in the church?

This a large order, which cannot be fulfilled exactly. We have heard a lot about the changes in the church in the past twenty-five years or so, and some Catholics think that the changes are over and we have settled down again. Whoever thinks that can forget it, for the church, a living being, has been changing since its inception. Most Catholics know almost no church history. I do not reproach them; the subject has been largely ignored in pulpit, press and school.

Today some Catholics are confused, dislocated, and unsettled. Others are exasperated, angry, bitter and stomping out. Some are vaguely floating around. (They remind me of one of my favorite desserts, called Floating Islands, a dessert made of white meringue "islands" floating on a creamy custard sauce.) Others are thoughtful and questioning. The old answers do not fit the new questions. One Catholic said, "The Vatican party line is not for this party."

Anne Quindlen, a *New York Times* columnist, wrote in the *Times* on January 3, 1991:

> Each year around this time, thousands of Americans come to church, looking for something. For some it is simply a search for some shred of childhood ritual, a past form without present belief. For those holding the hands of their children, it is often a search for that thing parents always want for their family, a direction in a world that seems without a compass.
>
> Perhaps there has never been a time when people needed words to live by more than they do now. Perhaps there has never been such confusion about where those words can be found.
>
> Many of us grew up in families in which tenets of church and state were simple: they were inviolate and clear, to be neither questioned nor modified, the stuff of which samplers and slogans were made.
>
> This no longer serves.

Good. It means that we must use the minds that God gave us. It may take some effort and be painful, but it is spiritually healthful. We will become fully human, not just be automatons or puppets.

Galileo (d. 1642) had to kowtow to church authorities who in their ignorant pride thought that they knew more than he did in his special field of science. He thought that the earth moved around the sun, but they knew better. Denounced by ecclesiastical officials and brought to trial before the Holy Office, Galileo submitted and recanted. Legend says that as he did so he mumbled, "But it [the earth] does move." Galileo agreed with Cardinal Baronius that "the Holy Spirit intended to teach us in the Bible how to go to Heaven, not how the heavens go." To deny one's intellect, a gift from God which makes us human, is not the way to heaven.

When a former editor of the renowned Catholic journal *The Tablet* (London) died in 1978, the then editor wrote that the deceased editor, Douglas Woodruff, thought that

> the Church was falling apart. For many others it
> was pulling itself together; whereas he must
> have been tempted sometimes to think that God
> was no longer on its side, there is now a
> widespread conviction that assuredly the Spirit
> indwells in a way that many worthies of the old
> theology have ignored.

It is heartening to see a layperson wake up and realize, "Hey, the church isn't something out there. It's here, in me. I am church. I am as much church as the pope." Of course, that brings a lot of responsibilities. Growing up always does.

"It might be said," wrote a *Tablet* editor,

> that whereas it has been the common view
> hitherto that a human being makes an act of
> faith in the Church for the solution of his
> problems, the Church now makes an act of faith
> in her own people for the fulfilment of her
> mission. Human intelligence and conscience are
> now to be trusted with a wider range and

Floating Islands

responsibility in the apostolate of the word and
deed, not necessarily dependent on
ecclesiastical status.

Or, as the newly enlightened pastor in the delightful
play *Mass Appeal* says in his Sunday sermon,

You have power. Use it. It's not only Monsignor
Burke's church—this is our church. Fight for it.
You and I and Mark [a seminarian devoted to
Christ's teaching being expelled from the
seminary] must be allowed to help shape the
thing that has shaped us.

To some extent we have lost Christ's resurrection to
the Easter Bunny, All Saints Day to pumpkins and
witches, St. Valentine to Cupid, so I was glad to see the
Hispanics (East Harlem is often called Spanish Harlem)
take the feast of the Epiphany to the streets.

Christ's birth to a great extent has been lost, in the
popular mind, to Santa Claus, but the Three Kings (yes,
they were not kings; folklore gets mixed in) brought
gifts to Jesus. The text under the large photograph in
the *Times* says, "The streets of East Harlem were transformed into a Nativity scene yesterday as the Three
Kings Day parade marked the feast of the Epiphany."

Good for you, you Hispanics, I thought. There may
be a little confusion about what you are celebrating,
but at least Christ is still in there. For I had gone into
Woolworth's to buy a Christmas greeting card for a
pious old Mexican woman. Among the hundreds of
cards I found only one, just one, that related to Christ.
All the others, even the ones in Spanish, referred
merely to "holiday" greetings.

Even the old familiar "dime store" had joined in the
effort to obliterate Jesus. Christ's saving act of the
Incarnation had become blah, reduced to nameless,
meaningless, no-think "holiday." Some cards had
"Season's Greetings." So the season was greeting us.

121

Which season? Winter, I suppose. Would Spring, Summer and Autumn each greet us in return?

I tried stationery stores. The results were the same. Except for one. It had one religious card and above it was the caption, "For Priests." My troubled face gave in to a wry smile: at least *I* existed.

Having given up on trying to find Christmas cards relating to Christmas, I watched on television a Midnight Mass at a cathedral. The homily of the presider, a cardinal, was so theologically deficient that I wished that he had had the humility to get help in preparing it. At communion time he, with his arm extended ramrod fashion, gave the ciborium to another priest to distribute communion. He then sat down. At the end of the Mass, he made politically tinged remarks to "honored guests." He thanked people for coming, as though the Mass were a production in which he was the star.

I should have known better, but on Christmas morning I decided to watch the TV Mass for shut-ins. The Mass for shut-ins, which most dioceses have each Sunday, is live. People at home pray along as the priest offers Mass in a TV studio chapel. "That's just a tape," said my friend, whose small children I had babysat during the Midnight Mass. "The cardinal (again the presider) taped that October 1, poinsettias and all."

"There was no announcement of that," I said. "The people at home are accompanying a tape. They are being deceived."

"Yup," my friend answered. He had helped with the taping.

What's a Catholic to do?

Grow up. Become more self-reliant. Look over one's spiritual life and see where one stands in relationship to God. Gripe, yes, and see what is wrong in church practice. Also see what is good, what is faithful to Christ. I saw an article today telling older people to "become more self-reliant in terms of retirement." We must do the same in our spiritual life—become more self-reliant.

No one person makes up the whole church. That's why "Will the church recognize my marriage?" is such a stupid question. Each one of us is as much church as the other. "Like living stones, let yourselves be built into a spiritual house, to be a holy priesthood, to offer spiritual sacrifices acceptable to God through Jesus Christ" (1 Pt 2:5).

We can look at our spiritual life and see what we have lost and what we have gained over the years. We must be wary of letting this world take over our lives so that we forget about the next world. "Mary has chosen the better part" (Lk 10:42).

"Let anyone with ears to hear listen!" says Christ (Mk 4:9 and 4:23). There are numerous times in the New Testament in which God the Father, Jesus and the evangelists tell us to listen. We must take the time and observe the silence for that. In the silence of the night Christ was born, and he can be born in our heart in the silence of spiritual reading and meditation. "Mary treasured all these words and pondered them in her heart" (Lk 2:19).

Thus we will be better able to evaluate the losses and gains, the good and the bad, in our changing, developing church and will be able to dispel our uneasiness and doubt in our practice of the faith. We will not let Christ, "the same yesterday and today and forever" (Heb 13:8), be replaced in our lives.

Reflection Questions

- If you are as much the church as the pope is, as Fr. Fehren says, what are your responsibilities?

- Fr. Fehren says we have lost Christ's resurrection to the Easter Bunny, All Saints Day to pumpkins and witches, St. Valentine to Cupid. Is this the case in your own life? If so, what are you doing to restore the balance?

- What can you do to become more self-reliant in your spiritual life?

NINETEEN

Company's Coming

"Why do you want to go to Antarctica?" my friends asked me. They looked at me as though I were crazy. "The bottom of the world. There's nothing there but cold and emptiness. No Hilton hotels."

"Because it's there," I would answer. And then add, more facetiously, "God made it. It is part of God's creation. And God made it for us. So God may be grateful that I made the effort to go see what God made. Having seen it, I could show god my appreciation and tell him that I'm much obliged."

One friend said, "Boy, you could rationalize yourself out of a mortal sin." So I told him that my real reason for going was to get away from that noisy Christmas card. You probably have sent or received Christmas cards that play a tune when opened. There is a flat, small, round battery attached. One of the marvels of this scientific age, I guess. Anyhow, I received one and when I opened it, the card started playing Christmas carols.

But when I closed it, the carols continued. What to do? There is no "off" switch. Stomp on it and smash it? No, that would be sacrilegious, I figured. After all, it is a Christmas card, something somewhat sacred, and it is playing religious music. "Get thee behind me, Satan,"

I told my competitor. He would clap his horny hands if I showed disrespect to baby Jesus.

One solution I thought of was to put on a recording of Beethoven's Ninth Symphony and turn the volume up loud. Then I wouldn't be able to hear the tireless repetition of the same old carols. But then I couldn't hear the doorbell either. And the guy delivering my pepperoni pizza would leave since he got no response when he rang the bell.

Although I was fearful of being accused of lacking Christmas spirit, I commanded the card under holy obedience to stop. It ignored me. It probably was aware of a higher authority. And, as usual, the 1,752 rules in the Canon Law book were of no help.

So I fled, fled to the stillness and serenity of Antarctica.

The account of the non-stop Christmas card is true but escape from that was not really the reason for my Antarctic visit. The reason was somewhat similar, though. Perhaps because of where I live (in the center of New York City) and my variegated activities, I constantly meet Catholics or ex-Catholics who bombard me with complaints about priests and bishops, including the bishop of Rome, "official" church regulations, practices and some teachings not based on the gospels. The litany, like the Christmas card, is never-ending.

Perhaps the Roman collar is a magnet for these people; if so, I'm glad that it is. Or even if I do not have the collar on and they learn that I am a priest, they come to me. Perhaps I look non-threatening or lack an authoritarian mien. I'm pleased that they feel free to speak their mind and that they are concerned enough about their faith to discuss or at least to air their opinions, problems or what's bothering them.

"Cease and desist" I sometimes feel like crying out. I get the impression sometimes that these hurt, offended, disgruntled or merely exasperated Catholics expect me to do something about their grievances or they feel the need to justify to me their distancing themselves from church organization and ritual.

They not only tell of themselves, they tell about friends who have "left." "My brother had his kid baptized Lutheran because his priest was so mean and the Lutheran pastor was so nice."

"I supported that parish for forty years and now they won't marry my daughter."

"The pastor's sermons are sooo stupid. His elevator doesn't go to the top floor."

In Thomas Hardy's novel *Jude the Obscure,* Jude gives up on the church: "The Church is no more to me. Let it lie!" But they do not let it lie. They are bothered. And I'm glad that they are. The church in some way still means something to them. A letter in a diocesan paper says, "Our churches are dead, boring, and unfriendly, not to mention the preaching which is so bad these days and so unbiblical it has driven most people away."

Our separated brethren seem to have the same problem. A letter arrived today from a friend of the Episcopal persuasion. He writes, in reference to his Episcopal pastors, "For forty years we have suffered from a variety of duds—nearly all *bad* in a variety of ways."

Anyhow, Jesus felt the need at times to get away from the crowds and even from the apostles and went off by himself into the quiet of the desert. If Jesus can escape the pressure for a little while, I rationalized, I also can, and off I went, way off, to the stillness of Antarctica.

How was it? I thought of Psalm 23: "He makes me lie down in green pastures; he leads me beside still waters; he restores my soul" (vv 2-3). Not green this time, but white—vast expanses of snow and ice refreshed my soul. The magnificence of God's creation encourages faith and the tranquility of the whole scene calms the soul.

Even the penguins are helpful for, unafraid of people, they look naive and innocent as they waddle or jump around. Icebergs of all sizes and shapes, floating peacefully in the still water, are awesome and beautiful. No billboards, no roads, no TV ads, no radio, no pollution, no junk mail, no baloney. One could sense "the peace of God, which surpasses all understanding" (Phil 4:7).

I made only one mistake. No, I did no slip on guano. I brought along a copy of Axel Munthe's book, *The Story of San Michele*, which friends of mine in Buenos Aires had given to me.

The book contains the spiritual reflections of a retired doctor as he builds a home on the isle of Capri. It's a very good book, but published in 1928 and long out of print, I suspect. And, sure enough, there is a complaint about a priest: "Don Giacinto himself, the richest priest in Capri, who had never given a penny to the poor, is still roasting in his coffin." What I left home to avoid for a while was staring me in the face.

So when I got home I went to a concert of Mozart's religious music. Classical music concerts are another way of escape from people with horror stories of the church. And the concerts are a gift from God. I don't have a critical ear, so if the music critic the next day says that the soprano was flat, it is too late. I have already enjoyed the concert. But this time, here it was again: the program notes revealed that the Mozart family, good Catholics, "were frankly critical of corruption in church hierarchy." When the tyrannical Prince Archbishop accepted Mozart's resignation as a church composer, he had him physically kicked in, ah, his rear end.

If the complaints of clerical abuse are genuine, I side with the people. It is the honest thing to do. Sometimes they are surprised. But St. Paul said, "Weep with those who weep" (Rom 12:15). He didn't tell us to cheer them up.

I think that most priests are doing the best they know how, but when things are going well we do not hear much. When things go wrong, that's when the noises are made. Still, one woman gushed to me, "Oh, Father, we have the most wonderful Monsignor!" Glad to hear it. I'm sad, though, when people avoid Mass because of some priest or bishop. We go to church to worship God, not the priest.

"Rejoice in the Lord always," says St. Paul (Phil 4:4). The priest may be our part of the sacrifice we make in the sacrifice of the Mass, but Jesus is always there. So we will be. "Come to me, all you that are weary and are carrying heavy burdens" (Mt 11:28).

I get tired of those who say, "I get nothing out of Mass." Perhaps they give nothing. Christ on the cross did not ask, "What do I get out of this suffering?" We come not to be entertained or pampered. We do come to be loved, for at Mass Christ gives himself to us. "Take this and eat." Christ could ask us, as he did the disciples of John the Baptizer, "What then did you go out to see?" (Lk 7:25)

Jesus put up with and still loved Judas, who betrayed him; Peter, who denied him; Thomas, who doubted him; the apostles, who abandoned him. "We who are strong ought to put up with the failings of the weak," says St. Paul (Rom 15:1). This is not to excuse any wrongs or abuses in the church; St. Paul also reminds us that "we will all stand before the judgment seat of God" (Rom 14:10).

On the way home from Antarctica I stopped in Ecuador. A tour guide in Quito showed me the "church of the Company of Jesus." He was referring to the Jesuits, for that is what St. Ignatius called his group. Lovely, I thought; at Mass especially we are the company of Jesus. As a child I loved it when my parents announced that "company's coming."

In those days guests came well dressed as a mark of honor to the hosts. Today some parents come to Mass dressed as though they were going out to slop the hogs. Children will not see Mass as important unless special preparation is made to be the guest of Jesus. Jesus made preparations for the Passover supper (Mt 26:17-19).

The letter to a diocesan paper which I quoted also had this statement: "Why I stayed in the Catholic Church so long is solely because of the Eucharist." A wise person. On Sunday morning we don't want God out looking for us as he did for Adam and Eve, asking, "Where are you?"

Reflection Questions

- Have you ever said, "I don't get anything out of Mass?" Fr. Fehren suggests that people who say this may be looking to be entertained. Is this criticism valid?

- If Christ asked you, "What did you go out to see (at Mass)?" how would you answer?

- "Today some parents come to Mass dressed as though they are going out to slop the hogs," says Fr. Fehren. How do you dress for Mass? Does this say anything about your attitude toward the celebration?

- Does thinking of Jesus as "company" help define how to behave at Mass? If so, how?

TWENTY

Will the Real Jesus Christ Please Stand Up

I am not sure it is running anymore but there was among the TV quiz shows one in which the contestants were to choose among three persons present which one was the character described by the quizmaster. The contestants could ask questions of the three candidates.

When the time for questioning was up and the contestants had guessed at the identity of the person, the master of ceremonies would say, "Will the real *(name of the person)* please stand up." Then the contestants and the viewers would find out if they had guessed correctly.

It could be interesting to be the subject of such a game—be lined up with two other people not Catholic and have the contestants guess which one is the Catholic. Their questions would have to be limited to the kind of life we lead, how identified we are with Christ in the kind of life he led, and whether we are clothed in Christ (Gal 3:27).

How would anyone discover that I am a Catholic or identify me as a Catholic?

Some years ago contestants might have asked, "Do you abstain from meat on Friday? Do you attend the Perpetual Help devotion every Tuesday? Do you have a St. Christopher medal in your automobile? Do you keep the Nine First Fridays? Do you take part in Tenebrae services? Do you have a rosary in your pocket or your pocketbook? Do you have several medals (of Jesus or the saints) on a chain around your neck? Do you make novenas? Do you give up candy for Lent? Do you go to May devotions? Do you make the Stations of the Cross? Are you wearing a scapular? And, depending on whether you are a woman or a man, do you cover or uncover your head in church?"

All these question bring on nostalgia for Catholics over forty, but even if one said "Yes" to all of them, one might hesitate to stand up when the MC said, "Will the real Catholic stand up." And even if one could say "Yes" to all those questions, a Catholic might get slightly scrupulous and ask, "Do those things make me really a Catholic? Am I really a Catholic? What makes a Catholic a Catholic?"

We could do the things listed above and still not be a Catholic at heart, a real Catholic. We could do them and still be a surface Catholic, a superficial Catholic. So then we ask what makes a real Catholic. A Catholic is a Christian, a person who identifies with Jesus, who has the mind of Christ (1 Cor 2:16). To say, "Will the real Catholic please stand up," is almost like saying, "Will the real Jesus Christ please stand up." Not quite, though, for Jesus is his own person and we are not clones or carbon copies.

Christ, his mission given by his Father, had his particular work to do and we have ours. John the Baptizer's life was so Christlike that he had to point out that he was not Christ but was sent to prepare for him. Jesus left "an example, so that you should follow in his steps" (1 Pt 2:21), yet each of us must do it in our own way, according to the mission that God has given us.

It is interesting that John, when he was in prison, heard about the works of Jesus and sent his disciples to ask if he were the real Jesus Christ (Mt 11:2-6). In other words, "Will the real Jesus Christ please stand up." Jesus told them to "go and tell John what you hear and see: the blind receive their sight, the lame walk, the lepers are cleansed, the deaf hear, the dead are raised, and the poor have good news brought to them."

Yes, he is the real Jesus Christ. In other words, by their works you shall know them. Has any acquaintance ever said to us, "Gee, I had no idea that you were Catholic"? Could it be that in our own way we have not helped the cripples, lepers, and the deaf or brought new life to people? This does not mean that we must be capable of physical miracles; the works of mercy will qualify. That is how God will recognize us on judgment day (Mt 25:31-46).

In Chicago on Good Friday, Mexicans stage a street pageant, a public Way of the Cross, in which one person chosen as Jesus carries a cross to a crucifixion site. He is surrounded by "soldiers," and thousands of people follow along. The Christ is even put up on the cross and there he "dies."

In searching for the man to play the part of Jesus, the organizers of the street pageant try to find a person in the community who in his daily life most closely follows the way of Jesus. The person chosen this year said that the role is a difficult one to live. "You live in the community and they watch what you do," he said. "You're really living the part you're playing." And thus it should be for all of us.

What does Jesus say? "By this everyone will know that you are my disciples, if you have love for one another" (Jn 13:35).

Love is not just a vague, philosophical concept. It is something that we do. We do not "make" love; we *do* love, as Jesus did. "Just as I have loved you, you also should love one another" (Jn 13:34). Lest we miss the point, he repeated that demand (Jn 15:12). He showed us how to love.

That love, of course, must be based on faith in Jesus and the teaching he received from his Father (Jn 12:49-50). To love is to be true to his word (Jn 14:24).

There are many examples of his love for others. He looked steadily at the rich young man and "loved him" (Mk 10:21). He loved Martha and her sister and Lazarus (Jn 11:5).

And he wanted love. Jesus, a man, was not ashamed to ask for the love of another man, Peter. "When they had finished breakfast, Jesus said to Simon Peter, 'Simon son of John, do you love me more than these?' He said to him, 'Yes, Lord; you know that I love you.'" Jesus asks again and the answer is the same. But Jesus needs reassurance; he is insistent and asks for the third time if Peter loves him. Peter, naturally, is hurt: "Lord, you know everything; you know that I love you" (Jn 21:15-17).

I don't like to clutter up the page with Scripture chapter and verse numbers, but to be Catholic we must use Scripture, especially the New Testament but not neglecting the Old, frequently—daily if possible. If we are ever tempted to give up on our faith, our life or our mission from God, we need to open those pages and read again. It is difficult, for instance, to read chapters 12-17 of John's gospel and not want to be a Catholic, a follower of Jesus.

Yet some observers sense that there is less of a Catholic presence in our social and national life today, that "discretion has become our watchword, non-belligerent faith our code." One writer says that though God by the Incarnation made himself visible in the human arena, we are more and more making religion a purely private affair.

To be sensitive to people with other-faith or no-faith does not mean that we must conceal our faith. Jesus didn't get lost in the crowds, vanish into the shadows or keep his faith behind closed doors. He went public about his faith and who he was. Could Jesus say of us as he said of John the Baptizer, "What did you go out into the wilderness to look at? A reed shaken by the wind?" (Mt 11:7)

Another writer says,

> We like a "thin" religion which has a few moral structures but doesn't carry us into the depths of who we are and who God is. Most parents today want their children to be "happy" or "secure," vague generalities which have become goals rather than consequences.

There are times when Catholics, because of the public unChristian action of appointed church officials, feel ashamed to admit being Catholic. Some expressed that feelings to me when a cardinal insulted a black mayor of the city in a St. Patrick's Day parade. The only thing to do is to join the secular columnists who denounced his sin (almost no Catholic paper or magazine will do that), forgive, as Christ asked us to forgive our enemies, and "pray for those who abuse you" (Lk 6:28).

The Mozart family was frankly critical of corruption in the church hierarchy, but Wolfgang Amadeus wrote to his father, "I also recognize God's love, his compassion and his tenderness toward his creatures." *Be there* as a Catholic, says the saintly Jewish Carmelite nun, Edith Stein. "Be present by the power of Christ's cross at every front, at every place of sorrow, bringing to those who suffer, comfort, healing and salvation."

"To do nothing for the community of faith, to do nothing that declares one's identity as a member," writes another concerned Catholic, "to do nothing as a member which is distinctive or demanding, all not only reveal but probably encourage a rather tenuous detachment."

Which is probably why Cardinal Newman said that the difference between an ordinary religious person and a saint is that the saint "is habitually striving to have a closer resemblance to Christ in all things."

So we hope that on the last day, when we are lying in our coffin, and God says, "Will the real *Christian* please stand up," we won't have cause to hesitate.

Reflection Questions

- If you were on the game show described on page 131, would the panel be able to identify you as the real Catholic?

- If a Catholic is like Jesus Christ, is there any real difference between a "Christian" and a "Catholic?"

- How would you feel if you were picked to play the part of Christ in the pageant described on page 133?

- Where does Scripture fit into your life?

Twenty-one

Good, Better, Best

"You will like the article about Marcia Davenport." Marcia Davenport? Who is Marcia Davenport? The only davenport I know is a piece of furniture that seats three or four people. Today it is usually called a sofa.

I'll tell you. She is the daughter of Alma Gluck. There. Well, who is Alma Gluck? Her name sounds like a Minnesota beer no longer made—Glueck. She was a concert singer, the one most in demand in her time (d. 1938). From her Marcia Davenport received the desire and the resolve to strive for perfection, to do the best that she possibly could in whatever she was doing.

And that is why a friend sent me a copy of *New Yorker* magazine with a lengthy profile of Marcia Davenport, who, then eighty-seven, "has spanned the realms of music and literature for more than half a century." My friend knew that I consider doing one's best as a means of holiness. That may sound a little trite or corny, but that does not make it less true: God has given each one of us different gifts and we are expected to use them. Otherwise we are scorning what God has given to us.

"Marcia Davenport," said the article, "may well have spoken and written about the singing voice longer and with greater precision and critical expertise than anyone else alive." How did Marcia achieve such perfection as a music critic? She used the brains God gave her and she used them to the utmost. "Genius," said a genius friend of mine, "is one percent inspiration and ninety-nine percent perspiration."

A friend of hers called her "a relentless purist." She learned the ideal of perfection from her mother. "My mother," she recalls, "was very, very particular about how one spoke and about one's voice. If I said something and my voice wasn't right, she'd say so." She preferred to be fastidious rather than sloppy in anything she did. In New York Marcia attended *every* rehearsal of Toscanini's orchestra. "It was a process of adding to the mass of authentic knowledge that I knew would stay with me all my life....I learn, I learn, I learn."

We hear on all sides today that the quality of life has gone down—that things aren't made the way they used to be. Everything made is junk, designed to quickly fall apart or deteriorate. Cities have reached a crisis in trying to find landfills for trash. Quality is an outdated concept. A friend of mine was offered $45,000 cash on the spot for his 1973 Cadillac. "Cars aren't made that way anymore," said the would-be buyer. My friend preferred the car to the cash.

Marcia thinks that she "was born and reared among giants in a world that is now largely inhabited by Lilliputians." I am unqualified to make that judgment, but I do know of many, many instances where Rembrandt is replaced by Andy Warhol. When Marcia brought the beginning of her first book to Max Perkins, one of America's greatest book editors, he said, "Go ahead and write it. We will publish it." When asked about such confidence, he said that he could see that "she was unconquerable and would do what she undertook."

At least in editing I have seen a decline over the years. Book publishing companies have been gobbled up by corporations who hire freelance editors, since it is cheaper, rather than have inhouse editors. (Yes, in recent years even I have suffered from copyeditors lacking humility and competence.) Maybe the fast food mania affects many fields of endeavor.

But, as a noted poster says, "God made me and God doesn't make junk." The parable of the talents (Mt 25:14-30) lets us know that God expects a return for the gifts God has given us. In reference to the man who buried his talent, we sometimes forget the conclusion of the parable: "Throw him into the outer darkness, where there will be weeping and gnashing of teeth." Everything we do should be in response to our calling from God. We do not want to do something slipshod for God.

Unless the Lord builds the house, we pray in Psalm 127, they labor in vain who build it. We work with God and it is not likely that God will deliberately do shabby work. We used to measure our piety by counting prayers and acts of self-denial, but theologian Fr. Karl Rahner says that "Christian asceticism must not be governed by conscious or unconscious contempt of the world, unfaithfulness to or flight from one's earthly duties."

It is false asceticism, he adds, "to despise the world because one is too weak and too cowardly to grapple with it and master it in both its grandeur and gravity."

St. Francis de Sales agrees with him: "If a man does not perform the grave obligations of his state, though he raise the dead and practice all manner of austerities he is in mortal sin and will perish eternally." Our state of life is the vocation to which God calls us and God calls us to perfection.

We may have read of Christ telling us that we must "be perfect...as your heavenly Father is perfect" (Mt 5:48) and decided that it was impossible. We could not be perfect as God is perfect. Later Scripture scholars say that it means that we must be true or whole, that we are to be like God in God's love for us. If we are to be "whole," we must be as God meant us to be.

If we do not yearn for and work for excellence in our lives, we esteem ourselves less than God does. Laziness, timidity, indifference or lack of faith can prevent us from being all that God created us to be. Meanwhile, nothing that we do is indifferent to God. "So, whether you eat or drink, or whatever you do," says St. Paul, "do everything for the glory of God" (1 Cor 10:31).

What an amazing man Paul was! What courage! He probably never dreamed that he could accomplish all that he did. Undaunted by human and natural enemies, he made those fantastic and dangerous journeys — for God and God's people. As God knocked Paul to the ground to get him started (Acts 9:4), God may have to shove us off our easy chair to get us moving.

Paul should have been dead many times but God was with him — as God is with us when we overcome our inertia and timidity. I know from experience. A peasant must stand a long time on a hillside with his mouth open, says a Chinese proverb, before a roast duck flies in.

"Get up," Jesus told Paul (9:6), as he does to us. Then Jesus in a vision called a disciple in Damascus named Ananias. "Here I am, Lord," Ananias answered (9:10), as we should. "Get up and go," said Jesus (9:11), and see Saul of Tarsus. Jesus can be very demanding at times. And you never know what Jesus is going to ask of us.

But Ananias was afraid (like us sometimes), for he knew that Saul (Paul) persecuted those who followed the way of Jesus. "Go," said Jesus (9:15). So Ananias went to see Paul and Paul received his sight and was baptized. It's never good trying to outguess God. One man lying under an oak tree in a pumpkin field thought that God had goofed in one part of creation. Look at those huge pumpkins hanging on that little fence, he thought, and the tiny acorns on that big strong oak tree. I would have that stalwart tree hold the pumpkins and the lowly vine the acorns. And then an acorn fell from the tree and hit him on the nose.

When Paul was baptized, he received from the Holy Spirit the gift of fortitude, as we do in baptism and confirmation. Without it he could not have accomplished all he did in response to Christ's call. When we are tempted to give less than all, he is a great role model for us. Like us, he was a mere human being—made in the likeness and image of God.

Nor does age excuse us from doing our best in all things. The word "retirement" does not apply here. "'Retire' is something insurance company executives do, with golf carts—not what I did," said Marcia Davenport at eighty-seven. I was happy to see in a diocesan paper yesterday a picture of a ninety-two-year-old woman making beautiful quilts for the poor. She was being helped by another woman, aged eighty-six. As the creator of the Peanuts cartoon says, "When we're over the hill we pick up speed."

I am a part-time insomniac, and sometimes late at night when I can't sleep and my eyes are too sore to read anymore (I'm a readaholic), I flick on the television set. By chance, for free, I have cable, so there are lots of channels. I am horrified to see how stupid and insipid most of the programs are. Yet people must be watching them or they wouldn't be presented. And I think of what a wonderful thing the mind is that God has given us. To neglect, waste or misuse that fantastic gift must be offensive to God.

I could never see a need for drugs. Just to explore the mystery and beauty and complexity of God's creation surrounding us is enough to completely fascinate our mind. And doing that is holiness.

> Take time to see the sky
> Find shapes in the clouds
> Hear the murmur of the wind
> And touch the cool water.

> Walk softly—
> We are the intruders
> Tolerated briefly
> In an infinite universe.

I don't know who wrote that but I like the sense of reverence and awe for what God has treated us to. With love God has lavished so much on us that we want to make the best use of it and be the best we can and love God in return.

Reflection Questions

- What is your greatest gift or talent? Could you be using it any better?

- Has anyone in particular inspired you to do your best or to strive for perfection?

- Is striving for perfection ever unhealthy? When?

TWENTY-TWO

The Terminal Bar

In New York City, across the street from the bus terminal, there used to be a scroungy bar called The Terminal Bar. The reason for the name is obvious, but I used to think of the term "terminal" in the way we think of terminal cancer—cancer which will end in death. So I thought of the bar as a place in which to have one's last drink, the last drink before death. The bar was so crummy that it looked like the last resort. In fact, some of its patrons looked as though they were on their last legs. (Don't ask me *how* I know that.) I think that the city sanitation department closed it down.

After writing an article every month for twenty-seven years for *U.S. Catholic* magazine, I decided that its readers should listen to other voices and I wrote my terminal or last piece (the last chance to drink of the wisdom of Father Henry Fehren in his tacky journalistic bar?). Anyhow, that last piece made 324 articles.

I admire the editors of *U.S. Catholic*, especially Robert Burns, who made the magazine what it is, for I pushed to the edge what could be said in a Catholic magazine and they printed it—usually. One pastor wrote in that "we had a public parish burning of *U.S. Catholic* because of Father Fehren's articles." When some of the material was printed in a book (*Christ Now*), another priest wrote, "I purchased Father Fehren's book for the pleasure of burning it." That's fine with me. I was just happy that he had the intelligence to buy the book.

I am reminded of the words of the American writer Herman Melville, who died over one hundred years ago: "Let any clergyman try to preach the Truth from its very stronghold, the pulpit, and they would ride him out of his church on his own pulpit bannister." That's a bit strong, but we still do not have a "free" Catholic press in the United States. I don't mean one that's given out free but one in which new and controversial ideas relating to religion and the church can be fully and freely presented.

Nor, often, is one allowed to report what is really going on in the church. Many years ago I gave a talk, by invitation, to a regional meeting of the Catholic Press Association. I said that there seemed to be two churches, the one reported by the Catholic press and the one experienced by people in the church. Things have greatly improved since then, but when I write for the Catholic press I always feel as if I'm on a tightrope.

Melville also wrote, "What I feel most moved to write, that is banned—it will not pay. Yet, altogether, write the *other* way I cannot." A writer for the Catholic press must learn to write within the ecclesiastical picket fence that surrounds him. Still, I am not complaining about editors. They know that they can be sacked if they do not conform.

John Paul II's latest encyclical, *Veritatis Splendor*, confirms this. Overstepping his rights as bishop of Rome, he alone appoints every bishop in the world and controls every word in canon law, in the new Roman catechism, taught in the seminaries and written in nearly every publication of the Catholic press. He has summed up or compacted into one person, himself, the "church" and the magisterium (the "teaching church").

Just yesterday a Jesuit priest from Munich, speaking of how European Catholics are no longer paying attention to Vatican officialdom, said to me that the church the pope is addressing isn't out there anymore. As Gertrude Stein said, "There's no *there* there."

Journals published by lay people (*The National Catholic Reporter*, *Commonweal*, and the London *Tablet*, for instance) are most free, for they do not have a church official breathing down their necks. *The Catholic Worker* is almost free in another sense — founded more than fifty years ago by Dorothy Day (may she soon be canonized — without the customary big expense — so that more people can learn about her); it still costs only a penny a copy.

When I was in the seminary (I was ordained over forty-four years ago), we were told that when we were priests we should be careful not to cause any *admiratio populi*. It meant do not disturb the lay people. We were told not to bother lay people with fresh ideas, with new developments in dogma, with a more critical examination of Scripture, with a more sensitive application of moral laws.

It was insulting to the intelligence of the laity, of course. If I recall correctly, the advertisement for Carnation condensed milk at the time said it "was from contented cows." As long as they pay their pew rent, keep the laity contented. *Noli turbare fideles* was a similar thing we learned: don't disturb the faithful. That attitude was expressed by most of the Catholic press — and we are not yet free of it.

But the faithful are disturbed today; we see it in the tremendous exodus of Catholics from the institutional church in the last twenty or thirty years. Even priests have left by the thousands. I use the term "institutional church," though there is only one church, a community faithful to Jesus. What many Catholics will no longer countenance is the gospels being replaced by *The Code of Canon Law*.

That book, in describing the position of pope, uses the word "power" seven times in three canons. "I do not mean to imply that we lord it over your faith," says St. Paul. "Rather, we are workers with you for your joy" (2 Cor 1:24). One recent book by a Capuchin priest says that "never before in history has the Church been ruled with the centralism with which it is governed today....Rome replaces an absolutely unprecedented legalism, hammering on orthodoxy at all costs, church law at any cost."

As I write this I read of another theologian being fired as editor of a Catholic magazine because he discussed religious topics Rome did not want discussed. Jesus came to disturb people. And the religious authorities of his day thought that they could obliterate his ideas by killing him. We know the result.

Another great theologian, Fr. Edward Schillebeekx, has just published a book, *Church: The Human Story of God*, because he was "concerned that in recent decades, and especially under Pope John Paul II, the Catholic Church was returning to the triumphalism, juridicism, and clericalism of the preconciliar period."

The Association for the Rights of Catholics in the Church is also worried: "The style and numerous measures of the Roman authorities," it says, "tend to obstruct our ministry and create either a climate of mistrust, of anxiety, of indifference and eventually, of leaving the church, or an equally questionable religious obedience to human laws."

After writing monthly for *U.S. Catholic* magazine for twenty-seven years, the editors asked me if perhaps I had a main message or a basic theme. Perhaps it is this, that I tried to get Catholics to grow up, to not be so obedient, submissive, and subservient, to realize that they are the church, that no one but God can put them out, that they are part of God's household, in which they have responsibilities.

I tried to get them to have more confidence in themselves, not to cringe and be compliant, to know, as Jesus said, that God had determined to give them a kingdom. Some priests deny marriage, baptism, and the eucharist to good Catholics. Marriage is a sacrament administered by lay people, not by the priest. For the eucharist, it is Jesus who invites and he lays down no conditions. At the Last Supper when Jesus offered the bread, his body, he said, "Take, eat." When he gave the cup he said, "Drink from it, all of you" (Mt 26:26-27).

In the church we priests don't own anything; we don't own God, the church, the sacraments, the Bible, grace, Jesus, or the Holy Spirit. The Spirit moves where it wills, and the Holy Spirit comes upon anyone in the church as much as on any priest or bishop, including the bishop of Rome. Mary was not ordained, yet the angel told her, "The Holy Spirit will come upon you" (Lk 1:35).

"The body of the faithful as a whole, anointed as they are by the Holy One, cannot err in matters of belief," says the Dogmatic Constitution on the Church of Vatican Council II. Over the years I have heard more and more complaints about the increasing authoritarianism in the church, but I have also seen the laity become more mature and independent.

Other words I hear about church officialdom are secrecy, hypocrisy, and lack of candor and honesty. But, increasingly, Catholics just give closer attention to Jesus, to Jesus who "is the same yesterday and today and forever" (Heb 13:8). People make the same request as some Greeks did of the apostle Andrew: "Sir, we wish to see Jesus" (Jn 12:21).

I encourage the making of a "holy rule" for oneself. Religious orders always had a "Holy Rule" to guide them in their search for perfection. As individuals we need one for ourselves, a plan for our spiritual life. Otherwise we bumble along helter skelter to that final day, the day on which we want to say, "I was glad when they said to me, 'Let us go to the house of the LORD!'" (Ps 122:1)

We make plans for almost everything else: going to college, getting married, buying a house, getting a job, etc. We ought to make plans for the only thing we will have left when the heart makes its last beat. The basics are always the same: reading slowly, slowly, briefly each day from Scripture or other spiritual books or journals. That leads to prayer, to indiscriminate love of God and neighbor, to the works of mercy.

And each morning we will ask, "What am I to do, Lord?" (Acts 22:10)

Reflection Questions

- Fr. Fehren says his goal has been to convince lay Catholics that they are the church and "part of God's household, in which they have responsibilities." What responsibilities come to you because of your membership in God's household?

- Fr. Fehren implies that priests *should* try to disturb Catholics. About what?

- Having finished this book, what spiritual reading do you look forward to next?

SCRIPTURE CITATIONS

INDEX

Resources for Healing and Recovery

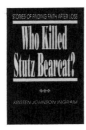  

WHO KILLED STUTZ BEARCAT?
Stories of Finding Faith after Loss
Kristen Johnson Ingram

Paper, $8.95, 0-89390-264-0

Nine stories encourage readers to find courage within themselves after a death or other loss. Reflection questions lead readers beyond the author's stories and into their own. Appropriate for grief ministry work, pastoral counseling, initiation groups, returning Catholics, or individual reflection.

HEALING OUR LOSSES
A Journal for Working Through Your Grief
Jack Miller, PhD

Paper, $10.95, 0-89390-255-1

The author guides you to record memories, thoughts, and feelings about loss in your life. Working through this book offers comfort to those grieving the loss of a loved one, and the process can help eventually heal the pain.

THE CHILD WITHIN
Music for Healing and Recovery
Julie Barrett Smith

Cassette $9.98, Songbook $9.95

This collection has many applications, from personal work to small-group work to liturgy. Ten songs include "Breaking the Silence," "Little Orphan Annie," "One Day at a Time," "Serenity," and "If You Really Knew Me."

Order Form

Order these resources from your local bookstore, or mail this form to:

QTY	TITLE	PRICE	TOTAL

Subtotal: _____

CA residents add 7¼% sales tax
(Santa Clara Co. residents, 8¼%): _____

Postage and handling
($2 for order up to $20; 10% of order over $20 but less than $150; $15 for order of $150 or more): _____

Total: _____

Resource Publications, Inc.
160 E. Virginia Street #290-B6
San Jose, CA 95112-5876
(408) 286-8505
(408) 287-8748 (FAX)

☐ My check or money order is enclosed.
☐ Charge my ☐ Visa ☐ MC.

Expiration Date _____

Card # _____ - _____ - _____ - _____

Signature_____

Name (print) _____

Institution_____

Street_____

City/State/ZIP _____